THE
GLORY
WOODS

THE GLORY WOODS

Virginia Greer

a hymn of healing

Christian Herald House
40 Overlook Drive, Chappaqua, New York 10514

Copyright 1976 by Virginia Greer
First Edition
CHRISTIAN HERALD HOUSE, Chappaqua, New York 10514
ISBN NO. 0-915684-04-7
LIBRARY OF CONGRESS CATALOG CARD NO. 75-45858

MANUFACTURED IN THE UNITED STATES OF AMERICA

To my Mother
and Kitty
and Jerry.
An explanation, with love.

And to John, my love.
To Happy, my daughter
whose gentle presence
sustained me.
And to Winnie, my friend.

CONTENTS

"The mountains and the hills shall break forth before you into singing, and all the trees of the field shall clap their hands."

Isaiah 55:12

PROLOGUE

THE NEW HOUSE in the rural woods of western Mobile County was grand, with its seven rooms, three baths and inside laundry. Grander than anything we'd known in our life together in our small home on a quiet residential street in the city of Mobile, Alabama. It was the culmination of our pre-retirement threshold.

Yet even with its old brick, split-level grandness, it was not the house that held this enthralling magnetism for me.

I say for me. It was awesome for my husband: but through his eyes, his feelings, his senses. Even in this loving and joint adventure for us into a new and later-life way of living, I would not presume to say "we," in many things we beheld. Who can know truly what another is feeling, experiencing? This is the story of those first half-year months through *my* eyes, and my feelings, and my senses.

I certainly had no way of knowing that in a staggering full-sense-of-the-word way, I would ease into a new concept of life, into a for-the-first-time concept of death; that those first six months would prepare me, unknowingly, for my skirmish with a malignant tumor. Six months to the day.

No, it was not the new home.

It was the woods.

The woodland circle that embraced the oasis created by felled pines and oaks where now reposed the house. The massive forest, poplars and pines, wild cherry and bay, magnolia and maple, sassafras and gum, oaks both magnificent and scrub—forest in small circles wound through with circular drive, forest splayed by the house, forest spreading as far as eye could behold beyond the rear of the house, deep and tall and mighty.

And nestling in the lowland, a curving, singing, splashing little brook, small creek, stream . . . call it whatever the mind chooses, a small journeying woodland water.

It is the impact of this woodland, forest, woodage on me that is the subject under consideration. It is the power that drives me now, somehow, to share it for those who have no woodland, forest, woodage. That is, if I can articulate it.

For as with that most powerful emotion, love, filling and overwhelming us with feeling for our beloved, the words come hard. And no matter the surging ache to tell one how he is loved, in what magnitude, with what all-enveloping devotion, when the words come forth, they are never as adequate as the inspirited love which prompted them.

The small unfolding story I share—middle-aged city girl, bookworm who came face to face with small creatures and met new depths in the towering trees, the isolated woodlands. Who sat in isolated nooks in the woods, piecing and sorting and trying to figure it all out —I hope the words are as adequate as the inspirited love which prompted them.

TRANSITION

IN MID-FEBRUARY on our five and one-half acres of rural woodland property the sourwood trees were in bloom. On February 18, I had walked through and through the new house, as unfinished and raw as it was, feeling the future touch and brush me. Such staggering views from inside and outside.

On March 2 and 3, the only entry in my journal was, *Busy! In attic.*

And on March 14: *Still in our old house, packing boxes everywhere. . . . How nice to open a kitchen cabinet and see only enough dishes for John and me. Why does one accumulate enough stuff for serving an army and let it make you a prisoner of keeping it. Someday when I am rational, I will give everything away.*

On a moonlit night in March we drove out to the unfinished house and sat on the patio in the moonlight. My husband and I. And felt the unbelievability of it all. Heard the soft screech owl and night peepers, frogs in the lowland across the brook. Viewed the gyrations of lightning bugs in the black forest.

Each evening as soon as John got home we would drive the twelve miles out to the unfinished house. We would sit on the patio, drinking hot spiced tea in the moonlight. (The electricity was on, the kitchen stove built-in.)

The screech owl, lowland spring frog chorus and lightning bugs in the deep tall timber seemed to be heralding our coming with an enormous symphonic warm-up. And through the trees we heard the traffic and watched the faint flickering of cars in the far distance going up and down hill.

Already it was as if we lived there, had lived there, all our life, and that no previous life ever existed.

March 23. Frustration. We'd been promised the house before April first. Interminable delays. Ready to move. Hurry up and do nothing. I turned to books. Books are good for renewing your perspective. Tolstoy's Romance of Marriage *and Smith's* The Christian's Secret of a Happy Life.

March 26. Went out to house at 3 p.m. Joyce and Jim came, brought hot mincemeat pie. We had coffee, pie on patio. Much enjoyment.

Jim was not feeling well, seemed discouraged. He told John he guessed he was lucky to be alive.

March 28. John got early (for July!) birthday card from my Mother calling him "the Cadillac of the people industry."

March 29. In mail in rural box, birthday card from my Mother to me: "While you celebrate your birthday/Remember old Granny's words of advice/ Grab all the kicks you can, Baby/ You only make the scene once."

And from my sister: "Another birthday and you're still the picture of youth/ A little retouched maybe, but still a picture!"

Easter, April 2. Sandwiches, etc., in house. Remains of March 30 birthday cake. Dogwoods, violets blooming. New green growth throughout the woods.

April 6. Closeout day. All complete, all financial legalities finished. Ready to move. . . .

THE MOVE

THE MOVERS ARRIVED at our home in the city at 9:30 A.M. They would move only the large items. John and I would take his last week's vacation and move the lesser pieces and the accumulation of all the years from the small house we had built in the morning of our love. The house where our three children had grown up.

Low swift clouds threatened throughout the day. But there was no rain. The movers worked smoothly. As quickly as they placed the small organ in the living room of the new house, I sat at it and played hymns and wept in sheer gratitude. The movers and my husband continued working steadily in other areas.

It was a miracle: the vibrato on the organ worked. It had been on the blink, off and on for over a year, fitful and unpredictable. John said the music sounded so beautiful from down in the basement, booming and resonant.

We borrowed a neighbor's trailer for hauling our other possessions. It would take forever. It had taken forever to assemble them. That day we drove back and forth the twelve miles from our old house to our home in the woods, John in our good car and I in my old faithful '57 Ford. We were in bed by 10:30 that night.

As tired as we were, it was a honeymoon-like life we

were entering. We were lying there, in our second story bedroom, entering that blessed state of sleep when I heard a scream. A woman's scream.

The scream lasted perhaps three seconds. It had spread through the deep woods seeming to come from the lower boundary which was rimmed by a blacktop road some 500 feet to the east of us. This section was totally obscured from our view by the impenetrable woods.

The scream ceased abruptly. John had not heard it. At least, he lay perfectly still. Later, he said that he'd heard it deep inside, even though he was asleep.

In the black stillness I tried to think whether I had imagined it. Surely not. It *was* a scream. I knew it was. But was it a woman's scream? Could it have been a wild-cat?

The woods weren't that wild, but we had, about a year before, from up the hill and far in the southern distance heard what we'd known to be the scream of a wildcat.

Even as I lay there in a fear-frozen immobility, grateful beyond words for my husband's presence beside me, the screams began again. Unearthly night-shattering screams, sundering the blackness, ripping it with terrify-ing ebbs and pinnaclings, the unmistakable screams of a woman, screams spreading, inflaming the woods with terror. They endured possibly three full minutes.

Our house was built at the very back of our property, five and one-half acres. The densest and most impene-trable woods lay between our house and the outer road from where the screams seemed to come. Our property could not be entered from that stretch of road, only by a side road far from the road of the screams. Lights in our house would not have been seen from that road. Our house itself couldn't be seen from the road. We had no phone. Our nearest neighbor was seven acres away. The incident occurred so swiftly, it was almost as if it never happened.

John, now bursting into consciousness, jumped up and ran to the double glass doors of our bedroom (where someday we hoped to have an upper deck). I was quickly beside him.

Instantly there was the roar of a revved-up car engine assaulting the black night. Then car headlights faintly pierced the far distant hill and blasted out of sight. Leaving the world to John and me. And silence. And no phone. And such a feeling of isolation and helplessness. In our deep acreage of woods and the unknowns that dwelt therein, our house deep in the woods half-way up a hill, it would be months before we had a phone. Always promises. And complications.

We went back to bed, disturbed, certain it had been the screaming of a woman. I felt desolate knowing there was a phone plug beside our bed, unconnected, no phone. Thus the evening of the first day.

The next day the organ would not work on vibrato; on the blink again. That it worked the first day must have been part of the total miracle of moving into the house.

We began again, that "moving," twelve miles to the old house, twelve miles back to the new house, carrying, lifting, placing endlessly. It would last for seven days.

That morning we looked for a "body" down by the creek culvert on the road. Cautiously, expectantly, because the nightmare had been real. The screams had not been imaginary. There was nothing in sight. No body. We went on with the moving.

That afternoon, Saturday, my friend Della came bringing, as she called them, silly gifts. They weren't silly at all. That night, Christie and Brad, our daughter and son-in-law came bringing a beautiful gift, a brass compote dish. We told everyone about the screams in the night, and our helplessness with no phone, and pitch black darkness.

We murmured over the mystery, shuddering in memory of the screams of terror from a nameless woman.

By Tuesday we had removed everything from the old house. We had stripped the attic where our son had grown up and reigned in his own realm of collections and paraphernalia of a little boy growing into adulthood. We boxed up and would house all three children's collections and acquisitions until such time as they wanted them for themselves.

Suddenly, the small house looked so spacious, stripped of belongings!

John vacuumed the attic and I cleaned woodwork in every room. Then came the mop and bucket. I cleaned all kitchen cupboards, doors, walls, and scrubbed the kitchen floor on my hands and knees, then mopped it twice. How it glistened and shined, the whole house. Refrigerator, stove, hot water heater, sink and countertops.

Exhaustion tore at me. I went into the air-conditioned lavender room, which I had used as a study since the two daughters had long since left for their own homes.

I lay on the floor in the empty room, aching from exertion. Limp. The pale purple ceiling, pale purple walls, pale purple drapes. I felt the house moving into me.

In the cleaning I had touched and moved and felt with

my hands and whole being, every cranny and surface of this house we'd lived in for over 25 years. My own personal farewell to this house.

I was so tired. My hands were swelling and my arms were puffing, as we continued our unloading of garages and John's workshop and sheds out in the backyard where our children had played and romped into adulthood.

Those sheds and garages had garnered their share in the years. I helped John with this unloading. It began to seem endless.

As we left our new home each morning during that week after we'd moved in, we shut everything from our minds except the removal of our belongings from the old house to the new. We would not officially be in the new house until the door was shut firmly on the past.

We would haul it, load by load, to our house in the woods, pile it in and go for another load. The books alone that I'd accumulated would stagger a library. The double garage was piled high with everything and so were the rooms above. It is a truism that he who travels light, travels fast.

For two more days we worked furiously at the old house. Then we called a junk man to haul off the residue.

Finally came the last day there. While John called to have the telephone disconnected and made a final report to the realtor, I walked through the empty house. My steps resounded hollowly on the floors. I sat down on the floor in the living room.

Outside, the yard was a splendor for the new people who would be moving in soon. Umbrella of wisteria blooming in great dangling lavender profusion just outside the backdoor. Red roses blooming on the trellis and white sprays of English dogwood would greet the new tenants when they moved in.

John walked into the living room. He stood there a moment in the vibrant silence. Then he said, "Are you ready?"

In that little while of eternity that I had sat on the living room floor of the house we were leaving, I felt again the joy that had cascaded, bubbling down the mountainside of years in this house, this home. I knew the repose, the poignant repose as that of a haunting goodby kiss.

With each of our children, I had looked into the face of goodby, departure from the nest. With each farewell there had been that repose, the letting go of a little of oneself and the inrush of a little of what one would become. To the end, becoming is the purpose.

I smiled at John, raised my arm to him. "I'm ready." He gave me a boost up.

When we drove out of the driveway, there was no turn of quick looking back. I was not Lot's wife.

HOME

NOW AT THE HOME in the woods, clutter invaded me. Particularly, the clutter of my study. Boxes and boxes of books that had to be shelved on the walls provided for them.

At last I had a room of my own to house my writing-related accumulation of the years. Known as "plunder."

I realized it was not clutter alone, but the sheer exhaustion from that week of loading, hauling, unloading and carrying in. We had forced ourselves from early day to far into dark. It was taking its toll.

A certain disorientation set in. Everything now demanded conscious effort to think before a move was made. Before, in a decades-long familiar place, about ninety per cent of what one did was by reflex. Even such simple acts as cooking, washing dishes, going to the bathroom. Now, the conscious-thinking effort seemed to drain. Not to mention that unending sense of boxes, disorder still awaiting the sorting and placing. . . .

Deep within me I knew it would all shape up with time. I tried to live receptively, with the sure knowledge that my life would evolve into order.

But one morning I was shaken completely by the enormity of the work ahead of me. All those past years seemed to be stacked up all around me, in boxes.

I hurried to the Bible. To Ecclesiastes. I knew there was something somewhere there about a time for each thing in its season. I read three chapters in the Revised Standard Version. Suddenly I felt a little easier.

Our dear Preacher summed it neatly after surveying the vanities of life, our strivings after the wind, when he finally arrived at his livable formula:

"There is nothing better for a man than that he should eat and drink, and find enjoyment in his toil. This also, I saw, is from the hand of God; for apart from him who can eat or who can have enjoyment?" (Ecclesiastes 2:24–25).

And so, I was content, even with my disorientation and the pervading sense of clutter.

I took enjoyment from the labor. Slow labor and fast enjoyment. I was not so upset by it.

I wrote a letter.

Dear Della,

I have no phone to call on, so will write. How can I tell you what your thoughtfulness did for me, for us, that first day after we were finally in . . . before the long haul.

It was as if some splendid open house of love had suddenly developed. In your appearance with, as you called them, "silly gifts."

They were not silly. Sometimes we call things silly when we are embarrassed by the spontaneousness of our actions, when we feel fleetingly that someone might not quite understand the action prompted entirely by loving regard.

So with paper towels bought suddenly because "they match your counter tops, pumpkin-colored," I've wiped many a spill.

And amongst all my clutter of boxes, there sits the bulletin board you brought, with purple posies on it. You were right, and how observant. My study writing-area tile floor does contain some of that exact blue-purple in the pattern. I hadn't even realized.

And the yellow and bronze chrysanthemums, and chocolate brownies. The mums only now are beginning to wilt after a whole week. It is as if they've been trying to tell me something with their steady, clear, undrooping beauty, like maybe, "Hang in there, kid."

More than for all the gifts to see and taste and touch, your gift of friendship that goes quietly on in its constant being, for that I thank you truly beyond words.

* * *

Successive company and guests dropped in all day that Sunday following the long-haul when we felt at last in reality we were in our new home.

Friends and relatives came to visit. They made casual suggestions or paid compliments or said nothing. I remember one woman said, "It will take a lot of work to keep this house clean; it is so big."

Strange, I had never thought of it in that way. The house and I would be comfortable together. I could bear (joyfully) to see dust on the furniture. I could always draw the drapes halfway (when we ever *got* drapes).

Among those who came to call were John's brother, Jim, and his wife, Joyce. Joyce was a dear friend, and I felt closer to her than ever, because the fall before Jim had undergone surgery. It revealed that he had cancer of the liver. It would be terminal, although he never talked about it, nor discussed it, either with his family or anyone else. If he discussed it with the doctor, it was strictly between doctor and patient. But it was as though he had never been told. We never really knew if it had been

9

spelled out for him. Even Joyce never knew.

Everyone played it Jim's way. He was sick, but had recovered from the surgery and was able to work in a restricted way. No one ever mentioned the real cause.

Between Joyce and me there had developed a large love. Following the surgery verdict, I had spent the night with her in Jim's room, while he was still in the recovery room.

Joyce had slept on a cot, and I slept on the floor. She had planned to sleep on the bed, and I on the cot. But that wasn't permitted. Jim's bed was off-limits to us, clothed in sterile linens.

So it had been a long night for me on the floor. Through most of the night, until almost dawn, Joyce had unburdened herself, her emotions, her fears, her hopes. Nothing was held back. I knew that it gave her temporary release, to vent her anguish. That was why I stayed.

But, on this Sunday night in April in our new home, Joyce and Jim were there. He was feeling rugged.

We told them about the first night in our house, about the screams, and how we had been unable to learn what happened that night, nine days before.

Joyce said, "I read about that in the paper. There was a woman attacked on that road. I never thought of it being the road in front of your property. There was a small item in the paper. Some stranger gave the woman a ride home from a public gathering. He attacked her on the way, drove off with her and let her out in another section of town."

There was the mystery of the screams in the night. Solved.

But it haunts me yet that we were unable to get to and rescue that desperate woman in those few moments before she was whisked away to another part of town and set free.

John went back to work the next day. To his livelihood, that is. His previous week had been hard labor.

Then, everything began to seem like a thousand Christmases to me. The big elegant house. The constant span of forest outside every window, spacious windows, for they'd been planned that way.

It was all too much.

And there began an enlargement of that sensation I'd begun to feel almost from the moment we'd bought the property two years before.

The feeling that friendly and curious little eyes were peering at me at all times, day or night.

WHIPPOORWILL AND RACCOON

IF YOU HAVE ever been serenaded by a lone whippoor-will at complete nightfall, you have known serenading. I never had.

A clear keen crystal slicing, "whip-poor-will," with emphasis on *whip*, with *poor* and *will* coming close onto, bringing up the fillip of the clear whisking *whip*. Into the deep woods the sound comes suddenly, the reverse of the dark somber brooding woods.

Night bird hidden, the sound surrounds, behind you, then to the side of you, then to your front, next to the other side, thence behind you.

Bird unseen, has leaped and frolicked and bandied and teased you, anonymous bird, unseen but present roundly and soundly, with that night-slicing *whip*poor-will. Pause of night silence, still, night of quiet, then shirring. *Whip*poorwill.

As though he and the night dark are dueling in a circle of woods circumferencing the house clearing. Not he, but the rapier of his voice *(En garde! En garde!)* and the night's experienced rejoinders, slicing, receiving. Clarion, sharp, air-piercing in a knifing undulation. He never ceases except for the pause after each thrust of brisk, clear slicing sound, fluid yet unbending.

* * *

I wonder if I will ever get over the wonder of this place. The presence of God's abundant nature always just a whippoorwill's call away fills my being with some responsive vibration that surely must have been resident from the day of my birth.

It is probably the human condition of reaching for truths that exist and elude us because we cannot fathom the unknowable.

Yet somehow the complexity of the simple that abounds in these mammoth trees, the community of birds, the fraternity of animals (we see their tracks), the territories of snakes, the diurnal movings of all these beings—the enormous simpleness and profound beauty stagger the soul.

It sends one to the psalmist and poets who felt and knew these things long before I.

But each of us is as surely a new discoverer of truth when it dawns in dazzling illumination as if no discoverer had preceded us.

And each shall look and view and take in at his own pace. This is the slow and glorious illumination.

I remember one fall, voices on the wind of people stopped to view the vista from a paved parking plateau high in the Smoky Mountains on a blue haze-tipped afternoon. The mountains spread in an unbelievable undulating panorama stretching into three states, all within eyeview.

The mind and eye received the sight in stunned adoration. Yet within this infinite outdoor cathedral, there came on the wind the disruptive voices of people saying, "Oh, lookie yonder, see the snow on that mountain over there?" or, "Oh, look at the colors, aren't they beautiful?"

13

Dear Heavenly Father, snow on a distant crest must be taken in for oneself. And there are some colors that take the breath in beholding, which are simply too awesome to be spoken of in mere tongue.

It is almost as if the human is embarrassed in the face of such overwhelming beauty of creation and must make little sounds to break the silence.

Their voices jarred me momentarily. Then I put them from my mind in the wonder of it all, and heard them no more. The sensibilities sometimes are the salvation in the receivership of beauty.

And so it is here.

This morning I actually said, "Good Morning," to a frog I could not see! The frog greeted me with a happy chug from down in the swamp beyond the dirt-circle drive. I was meandering after walking down to the far driveway entrance to bid John goodby. I said a second good morning to the frog on my return trip.

It sounded so good and not silly at all to offer friendly good greetings to a frog. He's my neighbor.

Yesterday I sat at treetop level in our bedroom in a rocker by the sliding glass doors. A marvelous large yellow bird, I do not know his make or model, flew into the dogwood branches, not five feet from me. I paused in my buttonhole sewing. I remained very still until he winged off.

Earlier in the morning as I sat on the patio, I watched two squirrels cavorting in pursuit of each other around the hollow hole of a four-forked towering bay tree rising from the creek and lowlands. Yet from the raised patio, the squirrels and I were almost eyeball level. Again, I stayed very still.

Again, I say. For this is their land. I am the interloper.

14

I must blend into their world and they will delight me with theirs.

Even the enormous fat black Eastern racer snake I surprised yesterday sunning on a brush pile brought me delight. *He* also surprised *me*. I was delighted that I did not scream. Oh, faint of heart to see the forest owners.

I saw his giant round middle, not slim, even corpulent. I saw it instantly, enough to observe that snake as fat and ebony with a carved-like black design on his enormous body. Before which, with singular haste for one so obese, he slid like water down a drain into the brush pile, out of sight.

The house is still a-clutter, islands of order surrounded by oceans of disorder. We still haven't hung drapes. More boxes wait for sorting and emptying.

And we have no phone yet. All is wild.

This morning we saw distinct tracks of an armadillo down by the driveway, leading across the road into another man's swamp. Wonderful! Along with raccoon tracks.

And something has been eating little Bruiser's outside tray of dogfood at night. We aren't sure whether it is a stray cat or dog. Or a possum.

* * *

Our house is a dream come true. It was all John's vision, his dream. A split-level house sitting just on this spot in the woods. And that's what he got.

He said one day, "It would have been good, if we could have spent the rest of our lives saving every cent and buying bonds and have something to leave the kids when we die. But I just decided that we ought to enjoy some of it for ourselves."

So, we're enjoying, enjoying.

15

Last Friday about 5:15 P.M., I was in my study. I was standing on the couch by the window holding up a drape to see how the new draperies I'd bought that day would look when we got the rods up. I happened to glance downward through the undraped part of the window toward the ground beyond the kitchen patio. I was on the second floor looking down. And behold, I saw an animal hunched on all fours—completely at home in the broad daylight—calmly eating biscuits I'd thrown out that morning for the red birds.

I was enthralled. I dropped the drape, eased down off the couch and watched him a few moments from that window. He apparently had seen none of my movements, as he continued eating, glancing cautiously around every few seconds.

I went downstairs into the family room and peeped from behind the drapes of the double glass doors (drapes we'd gotten from Goodwill) and stood there watching him. I really could not drink in what I was seeing. I had been gone from home all day selecting new drapes. Bruiser, our little Toy Manchester, had been inside, so there had been no activity outside the house all day. Perhaps that's why the animal outside felt so brave.

He was quite large. I did not realize how large until he stood up on his hind legs. His tail, a gorgeous long fluff, was charcoal black with stripes of gray going round and round. His little front paws were dark dove-grayish and slight, compared to his muscular and broad rear quarters and hind feet which spread elongated like a man's foot.

All the while he was eating his biscuits in mincing, deliberate bites, he would glance curiously about, not in any panic but as if he wanted to be certain of his safety.

His nose was pointed, a quite black little knob, and I forget exactly what his ears were like. Pointed, I think, much like a fox (which I've never seen, although earlier we had found fox burrows).

But across his pointed little nose bridge, there spread the darlingest small yellow and black burglar's mask. That led me to believe it was a raccoon, having never seen one in real live living black and gray and brown color.

Suddenly, he stood up. A gasp escaped my lips, I was so transfixed. He stood upward, rising up slightly on his hind feet, raring up to his full height, about two and one-half feet high. His classic chiseled face and head thrust upward on his stumpy neck so that he could peer over and beyond the patio to any lurking danger.

And standing there upright, eating the biscuit still held in his hands, yet looking for danger, he looked exactly like a miniature kangaroo. I have never been so beguiled by anything in my life. By this time I had slipped softly into the kitchen and was peeping from the big window, so afraid that he would spot me from outside.

The double windows by the table in the kitchen where we dine, are almost to the floor and are six feet wide. You look out onto the forest rising from the lowlands across and beyond the small creek stream. This forest is ever with you from any room, and in any direction, in the entire house. Just a small oasis of clearing immediately surrounds the house.

The kitchen patio extends out six feet—being 20 feet long—and the family room patio extends to a 12 feet depth. The raccoon (I was convinced that's what it was) stood about four feet from the patio. I was right at the kitchen window, so that's how close I was to him.

It took him about fifteen minutes to eat those biscuits (in the manner of a gourmet, of course) daintily. Twice he stood erect, upright, throat raised, chin thrust forward, every fibre in him alert, all the while feeding on the bread.

The sight of him standing there as though God had sent him in those little moments to give me another glimpse of the glories in store for me . . . it was almost more than I could bear.

No one but me seeing it, wilting with the tender sight. I watched him the full fifteen minutes.

Then suddenly, he whipped about. His furry brown and charcoal tail flurried in a whirlwind. He disappeared in a flash over the bank of the underbrush-covered high enbankment that descends abruptly to the creekbank. Two giant pines, smaller oaks, dogwoods and sassafras are among the trees reaching skyward from that underbrush.

Christie and Brad had driven up. Their car at the upper curve of drive had frightened young Racky Raccoon away.

I told them about the raccoon, so hoping he would return.

When John came home, I told him about the animal. We had been puzzled, he and I. Something had been eating the bread we put out for the birds, and it wasn't always birds. And something had been eating Bruiser's food at night.

We could not tell whether it was a possum or a raccoon. We had seen both sets of tracks all over the place where there is clear ground, and at morning down in the driveway by the road. John recognizes their tracks, and I am learning from him.

The night before, John had deliberately set food in a manner that would force an animal to move a board to get at it. A little while later, the food was gone, the board had been moved. Hardly a bird, and at night. We finally decided it had been a possum.

All this, right outside the kitchen patio, mind you.

And then, that afternoon I had seen the raccoon. And was telling John about it.

When I told him how tall it was, he said, greatly skeptical (as though I were telling tall fish tales instead of tall raccoon tales), "*How* tall?" It was obvious he found it hard to believe.

I said no less than two and one-half feet. I measured how high up from the floor.

He said, "Well, it must have been a big one. They're usually smaller."

As it got darker, I kept looking out the kitchen window. I yelled to John, "Come here, *quick.*"

He did. And there, calm as you please, making himself at home looking for food (biscuits, no doubt), was a possum. He departed and returned several times before we went to bed.

Now, compared to a raccoon, a possum is an ugly little animal. His long pointed sniffy nose looks exactly like a pig's snout to me (admittedly a skinny pig's snout). There is something obscene looking about a possum . . . compared of course, to that gorgeous creature, the raccoon.

And the possum waddles creepily about, albeit completely at home. He crept all over the backyard (if you can call it a backyard), up alongside the patio and skirting the kitchen wall of the house.

John told me I shouldn't feel like that about the possum. That it really wasn't an ugly animal.

But I had the feeling that the possum would be returning. When all the time I kept wanting the raccoon to return. I yearned for that darling little animal, so new to me, to return and become friends with me, even if with a pane of glass between us.

Every day, all during the day, I have looked. And especially at the "appointed hour," 5:15-ish, have I peeked and peered and hoped. I have put out much bread and checked to see if any were missing or had been disturbed. I kept hoping that my friend would poke his pretty nose cautiously from the underbrush and come forth. Not a sign have I seen, despite my Gretel-strewing of bread, and all my intense vibrations urging him hereward. Not a sign.

Yesterday afternoon John came home and said, "I saw the biggest coon by the side of the road about three-quarters of a mile up the hill from us. It had been hit by a car. The biggest coon I ever saw."

I hope it wasn't my friend Racky. If it was, then John knows I was not exaggerating when I told him how big and tall and like a miniature kangaroo he was when he lifted himself full tall.

I couldn't bear to go and look at the stricken struck animal by the road. I can still see him beyond my kitchen patio sent there just for me. Me and Racky.

And maybe it wasn't my raccoon the car hit. Maybe it was his brother. Or his poppa. Or his cousin.

And maybe yet, that little nose will peak forth, leading his small hands, broad hindquarters, that glorious yellow-black striped tail. And most of all, that deliciously sinister black and gray burglar's mask.

I'll keep looking. And remembering.

Since we first came into these woods, I have had the feeling that little eyes are peering at me from woods and underbrush, from above and from below. I cannot shake the feeling.

And everything that takes place, occurs and happens, now that we are domiciled here, bears that feeling into something tangible. I *am* being peered at by little eyes. Even perhaps being assessed.

One thing I know. This is their land. We are the interlopers. We must adjust to them. Not they to us.

I get so engrossed with my feelings about what I see and experience out here in the woods that I sound rattled. A city girl in the woods.

My letters must seem dull and monotonous, so cataloguish, telling of the woods happenings.

Like dear sweet Annie Jones, so long ago, who would write to Mother at length about what all she had canned. She would list everything so that it made up her entire letter.

I can appreciate her writing about all that canning, hundred quarts of corn, fifty quarts of beans, sixty half-pints of fig preserves, endlessly. It was what she was doing, was living, was experiencing. It consumed her time.

And we write letters about what we are experiencing. To others it may be dull. It may even be dull to us. But it is what we are doing, what we know, and what we are. So, canning, or trying to comprehend the incomprehensible in all these woods . . . of such are my letters. Woe be to the recipient.

Our evening whippoorwill who slashes the silent night woods with his keen whiplashing, non-ceasing cry at nightfall and into the black night. Who surrounds us in all these woods . . . one whippoorwill.

A heart-tugging view of an afternoon coon. And the stealth of an evening possum . . .

Or even my *canning*.

How about a dewberry cobbler that I made from dewberries John and I picked down alongside the road fronting our side property, or siding our front property . . . depending on what you call front and side, our acreage being bordered on two sides by distant roads.

AMAZING STREAM

YOU ASK: What is an armadillo?

From the dictionary I quote (noting that *armadillo* is located just above *armageddon* in the book):

A burrowing, chiefly nocturnal, edentate mammal (family Dasypodidae) of South and tropical America, having the body encased in an armor of small bony plates. When attacked, some species can curl up into a ball, presenting the armor on all sides. The ova always undergo two preliminary divisions, resulting in the birth of identical quadruplets.

Unquote.

What it is, is an animal sort of like a turtle except that its terribly bony shell is composed of strips connected with a kind of webbing. The armadillo's feet hang down lower than a turtle's and he has a protruding tail.

We haven't seen *him,* only his tracks, with signs of the tail dragging also. In most instances, there are big dog pawprints also, as though he were being chased by a dog or dogs when he made his feet-printing, tail-dragging dash into the swamp. To escape that pursuing dog. (Not little Bruiser, who would probably give a "Yipe" and head for the backdoor.)

I find it fascinating that armadillos give birth to quadruplets. Marvelous, the variety of God's creatures. I wouldn't have known that fact if I had not looked for a definition of armadillo.

* * *

We also have a pet bream (pronounced brim) . . . which in case you might not know, is a fish.

This bream is located in the small pond (some three-feet deep), located just above the tiny waterfall John concocted with broken concrete blocks across the stream. The water gushes and cascades splendidly. You can hear its musical laughter clear up to the house.

The bream appeared quite suddenly. A lone she. John said someone likely threw her into the water (after having caught her, some fisherman) upstream somewhere.

John kept talking about going down to feed "her." I said, "How do you know it's a she. Maybe it's a he."

He knew. "It's a she because she has two black spots behind her gills. A bull bream doesn't have those spots, but has much color just under his chin."

So. There is our little Brenda Bream with her two beauty spots, waiting at all times for the approach of someone to feed her. She comes with a whipping little underwater swirl instantly to where we approach. And hovers, waiting. For she knows she will be fed.

John catches ground spiders (ugh) and tiny crickets and throws them to her, one by one. She snaps the water surface with a loud smacking noise that broadly ripples the water. Sometimes he tosses her tiny bits of cheese pieces (cooking cheese). She does not snap the surface for these, but casually gobbles them as they glide downward in the water.

* * *

There is the most amazing phenomenon about that small pond of gently flowing water that houses this appealing fish. Truly a transcendental quality. I discovered it one day and it simply staggered me.

Only about three feet deep, this shallow water surface catches the entire reflection and silhouette of the forest, vast beyond words. I was sitting in a chair beside the pond, staring into the water. I saw day disappearing into dusk. I saw the tall pines, great magnolias, behemoth bays, stunning poplars and massive vines of scuppernong, and water's edge ferns and low underbrush suspended there, all caught up on the surface of the water. I could see the intricate etchings of leaves interspersed with sky, there on the water.

I stood, in order to really look into the water.

And suddenly the most amazing thing took place. I was not looking into the surface of a small pond located in the footland depths of a forest, a pond only three feet deep.

I was staring downward into the depths of a ninety-five foot tall pine tree, an eighty-five foot magnolia, a gargantuan poplar tree whose leaves were quivering in lofty breezes . . . caught in that water. The depth of that three-foot pond defied physics.

It cannot be so. Yet it is. I recline on the chaise lounge there and gaze upward into the mammoth treetops, into limitless sky. I stand at small water's edge and peer hypnotically into a subterranean world, ninety-five-feet deep, caught, suspended in three feet of water.

Phenomenal.

As is this whole situation of living deep in the woods. To live here is to vibrate with it.

For instance. Today we woke to a slow steady rain, the first since we moved in exactly a month ago. It is May 7, our first month anniversary.

The pattern of rain reaching into and onto the enormous "beyond" of forest that rises silently to encircle us at all times presents us today with a total new and almost mystical quality. It is there, to be faced, examined, or simply accepted.

That is the one consistent element I've come to realize about this place. "It" will let you hold it in abeyance from your comprehension until you are ready to open yourself to its entry into your being. You can shut it out, ignore it, occupy yourself with other little businesses.

Yet, when you are willing, or disposed, to turn to it, it is there. Patient. Receiving. Giving. Someday I'll find a name for "It."

Meanwhile I think of it as the divine isolation diurnally unfolding.

It never waits for me. Nature doesn't. It has its appointed tasks and primordial pathways. But whenever I am ready for it, it is ready for me.

In the woodland isolation and with no phone, I would write letters to loved ones, walk down to the distant rural mailbox to deposit them.

One day there was a note from the postman when I picked up the mail. It said, personally scribbled on a scrap of paper: "You forgot to put up the flag for your letters."

But, flag up or down, my daily outgoing letters in the box were promptly cleaned out by the rural motor route man. Faithfully.

One Saturday I happened down to the box as the letter carrier arrived. It was a she. She told me she was our substitute postman and that she lived thirty miles out in the country.

"How do you like living in the country?" she asked.

(Our house was hidden from the road, hardly visible because of trees.)

"Oh, I love it," I said.

"Me, too," she said. "I love living in the country. I told my husband now we don't have to wear out the curtains hiding from the neighbors."

On my walks I made constant discoveries of little wild flowers. As with the rhodora, they had beauty as their excuse for being, there alone in the woods. And the selfsame Power that made them, sent me to them.

Now John had carved out, with aid of power mower and tractor, another little "other world" down alongside the small creek in the bottomland. . . .

Because it was reverenced over by sky-seeking tulip poplars, black gums, bays and pines, and umbrellaed by embracing dogwoods that formed a low canopy, I called it Dogwood Bower.

An ancient, dead bay trunk, encrusted with strange mushrooms resembling barnacles, rose like an old elephant's hind leg, just standing there. The upper half had long since been blown and broken off the trunk by some hurricane wind. It lay askew and mouldering in the small waters as they trickled and rippled in and out.

This hideous old giant, moss-touched and lichen-licked, this ugly old elephant's hind leg was so outrageously inelegant and uncouth in appearance that actually it was beautiful.

I would go down to Dogwood Bower simply to gaze on the beguiling leviathan. I even found myself wanting to discourse with it as though it were some sage old being.

One day my doorbell rang. It was a young college girl in blue jeans and jacket. She lived up the road around the bend, and on the upper part of our rural road about half

27

a mile away. She was lovely, gentle, and taking art courses in college.

She held in her hand an empty jar.

"Mrs. Greer, would you give me some of the white sand down around your creek? I'm painting a beach scene that I want to enter in the Art Gallery Art Fair next week-end. And I want to mix in some sand for realism. We don't have any white sand on our property."

"Sure thing," I said. "All you want."

And so, we walked down to Dogwood Bower. All the while she marveled at the woods, at the little wildflowers, the "sweet white violets," tender young ferns and velvety green mosses, and the thrilling isolation.

Then we came upon the huge old bay trunk in the canopied closure of Dogwood Bower. I pointed to it and said, "I call that my elephant's hind leg. Sometimes I come down here and converse with it."

She looked at the old tree trunk. Then she said seriously, albeit with a twinkle in her eye as she looked at me:

"Mrs. Greer, *everybody* needs an elephant's hind leg to talk to."

CONTINUUM

AND I WROTE to my mother, who lives in Atlanta.

May 13.

Dear Mother,

Speaking of our dear fish . . . that day that the rain began so quiet and soft and delicately . . . that turned into the biggest eighteen hour deluge we've had in Mobile. In town, streets flooded and water came up into people's houses. A couple of refugee centers were set up in schools.

However, we live in the county. Out here the red mud swirled and gurgled and swept madly downhill. The little creek (no threat to us, for it is so far below) got completely out of its banks in a couple of places.

The water fell so abundantly that the little pond where our darling bream resided, rushed and gushed and the creek waters below the small dam got up level with the pond itself. We feared what might happen to Brenda Bream in that rushing small torrent of water.

Sure enough. She has disappeared, victim of the rapid waters, carried downstream, no telling where.

So many of our little nature episodes here turn into a brief beginning, middle, and end. I guess that is the way of nature. All of it fighting its own manner of survival. But somehow, for me each little episode leaves a bright actuality of memory, something that really happened.

Mother, when you wrote your last letter to me, you began: "Dear Learned Swamp Child:

I really have to dig the dictionary when I read you. Now, if an armadillo is a burrowing animal, how do he leave tracks? Sounds as if he would travel underground like a mole."

Now don't ask me about that armadillo burrowing. He was solidly walking on the ground when he left those tracks. Maybe he does his burrowing down in the swampy areas. We saw his tracks (including tail) on the road and driveway leading to the swamp.

The raccoon has not been seen again, but we have seen his tracks. We definitely see the possum. He comes frequently and eats the bread we put out.

He turned down bread for awhile. But we flipped the back patio light on one night, and there he sat. Just blinked his rheumy eyes and kept on eating bread.

* * *

Forgive the small box of not-much I sent you for Mother's Day. I love you more than I ever let you know.

The day I mailed the package, I parked my car across the street from the drug store-substation post office, on a small hillside.

After I mailed the box, I decided to use the pay phone to call Christie. The pay phone is on the sidewalk in front of the drug store. I talked with her, then I went across the street and got in my car. I released the emergency brake then remembered I ought to go back and call my friend Janie and tell her that we had moved.

You have no idea how maddening it is not to have a phone. I feel so cut off from everything. Anyway, I was standing there *in the phone booth, chatting with her when a short, graying man came out of the drug store.*

He walked back past the phone booth. He paused and pointed down the side of the hill and said,

"Is that your car over there? It's rolling down the hill."

"Oh," I screamed to Janie, "my car is rolling down the hill, I've got to go, come when you can. . . ." Blam went the receiver.

My car had rolled down half a block, crossed the street and jumped the curb with the two front wheels. It was just sitting there, partly in the street. It was now on the same side of the street that I was. In the same state I was . . . askew. I was palpitating.

I walked down the hill, got in the car. My old faithful nondescript '57 Ford. The one of which a college student in my church training group once said to me, "Mrs. Greer, you have the only car at First Baptist Church it doesn't embarrass me to park my car by."

I backed my non-embarrassing car nonchalantly, "bump, bump", down off the curb and took my leave. By the time I got home I was a wreck.

I kept thinking of how busy that side street was, handling traffic as it does from the not-too-distant University of South Alabama. In fact, the new name of the street was University Boulevard. And how many cars go back and forth on it. And how, miraculously, my car had ambled on its own, driverless, down that half block, across and up the curb without hitting any innocent pedestrian or vehicle.

I learned my lesson about that emergency brake on a hillside and hopping out on impulse to go use a pay phone.

The car was fine. I was too, after I toned down. There is more to this rural living than meets the eye, Mother. Take care of yourself. Love, Jenny.

OF SNAKE-STALKING

I NEVER THOUGHT I would see the day that I, my children's mother, would stalk a snake.

I remember one time when our family was on a picnic outing and I was so frightened by the sight of a snake that our son laughed and told someone later,

"Mama was screechless with fear."

Yet, here I was, in the woods. And I knew snakes were, as you might put it, abounding.

Once, before we built, as John and I walked through the woods down a wide cleared path, we surprised the most gorgeous snake meandering along our path. John's soothing sounds to me—and to the snake—allayed my fears, and I was able (since John was right beside me) to really look at the snake. All black and scaly on top, the underside was red continuing into his waistline in lovely red scallops. I can still see in my mind those undulating waves of red and black where the two colors met. The most beautiful snake I'd ever seen.

However, John had killed at least seven moccasins in one location down by the creek over a period of two years. Those deadly pit vipers, the cottonmouth water moccasins. I shudder to think of them, much less to consider any contact with them. I gave them great caution and wide variance. Them I would not befriend.

But now residing in the woods, one day I sat in the small room just off the kitchen to the front of the house. In the house plans it was a dining room, but since we entertain in the kitchen, we'd made the carpeted room into a sitting room, with single bed-couch and sitting-reading accommodations.

I walked to the drapes to determine whether I'd heard a car come up the driveway. The house was so well insulated and being on a concrete slab, it was hard to hear the approach of a car up our drive.

No car in sight. But slithering slowly on the sidewalk fronting the house was a three-foot-long black snake. Just as jaunty as you please. I was starkly delighted.

Two-foldly so. He was outside. I was inside. And I was near enough to observe him safely. Not two feet away.

I knew he was a black snake, because the day I had happened upon that huge fat snake on the brushpile, I had looked it up in a nature book. I'd learned that it was an Eastern Black Racer. And knew, now, that the snake outside the window was a simple Black Snake. Beautiful. (Since he couldn't get at me.)

I watched him from behind the corner of the drape. I was transfixed. He was so magnificent. And so snakey.

Not a sneaky snake at all. Quite openly, he was exploring the premises. Our domicile, that of the interlopers.

As he left the locale of the room I was in, I hurried into the living room next door, and to the draperies there. There is a permanent set of hand wrinkles there where I held the drapes to gape at the black snake. (In fact, there are permanent wrinkles in four window drapes where this itinerant snake led me.)

In the living room I gazed at his journeying. The snake

33

paused in front of the wide living room window, raised his neck (neck?) up about four inches, gazed archingly and pivotally around, then flattened out again and continued sinuously toward the front one-step-up brick stoop.

There again, he halted, raised his neck even higher and cast his eyes hypnotically around. He then moved waveringly up the one step onto the stoop. I believe that he would have come right on in and joined me for coffee if the front door had been open.

I vowed right then never suddenly to throw wide the front door. Hereafter, I would hesitantly and slowly open that heavy door.

Then he slithered down off the stoop, onto the sidewalk, and then upon the brick planter to the left. This extends downward onto a graduated three-step wall leading to the garage and laundry room level.

I hurried down the interior steps and into the sunny yellow laundry room. I stood there at the windows, transfixed. I actually looked that splendid creature in the eye as he slithered down the brick step-down wall.

He moved with a Marilyn Monroe rhythm onto a green plastic garden hose that lay right outside the laundry room double windows that front the house. Again I stared, mesmerized, into that snake's eyes.

As he moved along down the length of the green garden hose, he went out of my vision. I flew back up the stairs into the foyer. I flung open the front door (momentarily forgetting my resolve never to do that very thing), stepped out onto the stoop and turned left, down toward the garage front windows.

I arrived just in time to see the snake's hindquarters slithering along the ground in front of the garage disappearing onto the blacktop 30-foot turnaround beyond the double garage doors, out of my sight.

I whirled back through the door, slammed it, turned the nightlatch, then tore up the stairs and through the hallway on into our large bedroom, lickety-split.

I shed my shoes, climbed up onto the kingsized bed and looked out the windows over the head of our bed, where the drapes serve as headboard. I could see the blacktop turnaround, and the black snake directly one story below.

From my perch, I saw the snake slither his way completely across that 30-foot blacktop and drop peremptorily down the embankment toward the massive hollow below.

I stepped off the bed, into my shoes. I ran back down the stairs and out of the house. This time through the kitchen back door. I hurried down the back grade of the yard and up onto the side embankment of the blacktop. Then onto the blacktop to the far edge where the snake had disappeared.

He was out of sight. I stood there, searching down into the distance with my eyes. At last I spotted him. He was moving into an enormous mounded brushpile, of which there were several. They were composed of huge tree stumps and angular smaller trees pushed over by the bulldozer that had cleared the forest for the house.

I watched the marvelous creature weaving up and down, threading through and over and in and out several of the craggy brushpiles. And then I saw he was causing the big leaves of a giant fern plant to tremble as he slowly disappeared into the lowland density. He was gone from sight. . . .

I sighed and walked thoughtfully back into the house.

35

Suddenly, I laughed out loud. I remembered something my mother had written to me long years ago.

It had to do with the world premiere showing of *Gone With the Wind* in Atlanta. All the celebrities of the motion picture were there, including Vivian Leigh and Clark Gable. A grand parade preceded the showing. Thousands of people lined the streets, including my mother who had come to see, not Vivian Leigh, but Clark Gable. And it was pouring rain, yet she persevered.

She wrote me afterwards, telling about the gala crowds waiting to see the Superstars. She added, "I bet Clark Gable would not have stood in the rain for four hours to see *me* pass by."

That was the way I kind of felt about the snake. Would he have circumnavigated woods and bushes and shrubs and trees to watch *me* perambulating the woods. I don't know. Yet I still felt that little critters and eyes were staring at me all the time. Maybe I was getting paranoid!

But, it was one little adventure after another. Impossible to be bored. Exciting and tranquilizing at the same time. If such is possible.

OF TURTLE-TALKING

ONE MORNING in mid-May, I was standing at the kitchen window, hands in dishwater suds. I was thinking of my mother, and wondering about my sister who was scheduled for gall bladder surgery in June.

I was gazing up the hillside into the woods beyond the pumphouse. The tall and stately sourwood tree was showered and resplendent with showy white tapering blossoms. And there, ambling down the small as-yet-uncovered ditch leading from the pumphouse to the house was a . . . I couldn't be sure. Yes, it was a turtle.

I wiped my hands on a towel quickly and hurried out to greet him. I was bigger and faster than he, so he offered no threat.

He took a quick turn away from the wild-flower over-grown ditch toward the center of the woods when he detected me. As I approached, he froze.

I wanted him to know that I was absolutely non-hostile. So I began to soft talk him, not really knowing how to soft talk a turtle.

He jutted out his black and yellow striped neck several inches, looking most gawky and awkward. He was immobilized apparently with terror as his black eyeballs rolled back to the corner of the sockets.

I was making all kinds of murmurings to him. I wanted him to know that I really cared. That I was not interested in obtaining turtle oil, not even to improve myself cosmetically.

I kept talking to him, saying things like, oh, "Don't be afraid there, little fellow, I'm your friend. You're a sweet little fellow (maybe she was a girl, I don't know), and I'm glad you're here. I'm not going to hurt you. Don't be frightened. . . ."

I accomplished what I went out to do. To determine the kind of turtle he was.

I had observed him and his little long legs and long neck of black and yellow stripes, his small size, high narrow shell of black and yellow uneven shell design. I had observed enough to hasten to the book.

I told him, "You go on, young fellow. I hope I haven't given you a turtle heart attack."

He may have been old; I don't know. Could be he was a little old woman turtle.

I eased away, looking back. He was still frozen solid. I went into the kitchen, to the kitchen window. I looked out. He was out of sight. Probably a frisky young fellow and not a little old lady turtle at all, considering his departure pace.

Then to the book. My woodsy bible. My manual.

According to the book it was a "chicken turtle." So called because it is locally eaten, despite its size (five to eight inches). Mine was about seven and one-half inches.

I certainly wouldn't eat any local turtle. They're friends of mine.

The day before, I had found a dead baby snake, possibly just hatched, outside the kitchen sink window, on the ground. The book said it was a "flat-headed" snake. It was champagne color with a black ring around its neck and a black cap on its head; about 10 inches long, and pale, naked blue-white on the underside.

I put it in a small jar (with help of a stick), and placed it in the refrigerator to show to John when he came home from work.

Every day I had some little adventure or other to tell him when he arrived home from work.

One day he brought me a bouquet of honeysuckle he'd picked from the far distant roadside embankment (that of the screams in the night). He also brought me three lemons (from the store) to make a pie for him. He was subtle.

NATURE, GOD, AND LOVE

WE SAW a big lone raccoon eating cracked corn one morning just past the crack of dawn outside the patio window. Fine and fat and fluffy and furry. I could not imagine a hunter killing such an animal, or any animal, for his fur.

Springtime ran lightly down the woodland path, willowing tulip poplar petals and budding maples. Wind and leaves joined hands and danced for joy, and singing laughter rang through the woods.

At eight o'clock that morning in the woods, a squirrel sat nibbling on a giant mushroom halfway down the hillside. Then he tugged the browned-biscuit toadstool from its base and scampered high up a pine tree with his treasure. He deposited himself on an outstretched limb in a sunny spot near the trunk.

Bracing himself with his tail against the trunk, and holding the huge mushroom against his chest like an autoharp, he set to eating. Around and around the big delicacy he nibbled, and shifted, nibbled, and shifted.

Easterly sun dappled into the woods, cast shadows and caused glintings. Red birds played shadowy chiaroscuro among the sun-toned branches. Meanwhile, the squirrel went nibble, shift, nibble, shift with the mushroom. Then suddenly he darted up the trunk, began leaping onto high branches of neighboring trees and disappeared into the deep forest. The residue of the mushroom lay in stilled evidence on the upper branch as if it had sprung there overnight by its own sporadic magic.

* * *

Someone has called time a "radiant and mobile medium." I found myself thinking in terms of the past. Precious memories. They linger in hidden remoteness, then bring a sudden unbidden leap of laughter, a poignant tear, to some otherwise ordinary moment.

In this woodland, among all the tall and mind-staggering trees, I found myself resembling that erstwhile squirrel. In exquisite and delicate small tastes, I was shifting-and-nibbling at the past.

It had to do with my husband and our three children and that small house in which we had lived together for so many years. And the part that nature had played in our daily lives. After all these years I was beginning to realize the pattern of nature that had threaded so goldenly through all those days.

It started seeping into me with the memory of something our son said to me when he was fourteen years old. It had left me speechless, and gone deep into my heart. I felt it was the one *uttered* thing in this world that spelled "complementary" for my husband and me, for our children's father and mother.

And that, in truly different ways, in polarization, we had given our children our own "natures" about nature. Different, yet unified.

* * *

My husband was born and grew to the age of ten on a farm in Kentucky. As a little boy on a farm, the world of nature was as much a part of him as breathing. And so, a kind of knowledge, feeling, first-hand experience became a part of his very being. An indwelling love of nature.

On the other hand, I grew up in a residential section of Birmingham. We had grass in our yard, some delicate pink roses and red-gold cannas, and a tree that grew beyond our yard. My contact with nature amounted to taking a bouquet of pink roses to my schoolteacher (coping with books and paper-wrapped thorned-stems enroute).

But there was something about woods that thrilled me. And to go riding at anytime with anybody and go past woods gave me a feeling I cannot express. A strange, beckoning, mysterious feeling.

And so, as it happened, on the very first "date" that my (future) husband and I had, one Sunday after church he and I and another couple . . . went to the woods! To pick tall purple wildly fragrant woodland violets, called rooster heads. And to take snapshots.

The rooster heads are long gone to wherever rooster head violets go. But the snapshots linger in our album, as do the radiant faces in those snapshots. And the precious memories.

Ah! The memory. Indelible. For in one particular snapshot, one "subject" was uncaught by the camera. My husband (date, boyfriend) had placed beneath the warmth of his sweater, a little lizard which he had caught and fingered tenderly.

"Here," he said, as he had held it gently out to me. "He won't hurt you. It's just a friendly little chameleon."

I backed away. I was not being friends with any lizard. Woods, yes. Lizard, no.

But the now-time-paled snapshot does not reveal the tiny terror I felt, knowing that that lizard and his little thumping heart reposed safely in the bosom of my soon to be beloved John. The snapshot shows only the joy and smiles that presaged love, love that does not fade as snapshots do.

I did not know it then. But I know it now. That little lizard was lying lovingly content beneath that young man's sweater. Also hidden in the picture is the beginning of my deep encounter with God in the world of nature. Here too is the hint of the love to bring forth our as-yet-unborn children. So much promise of the richness to come in God, nature, and love.

* * *

Our first little house was set in the midst of a large-sized (for that neighborhood) parcel of ground, seventy feet across the front and two hundred feet deep. By the time we moved from that home after our children were grown, the yard had become a breathtaking garden of azalea and shrubbery beauty. Handwrought by John and his love of working with the earth.

Five pecan trees, a giant five-trunked mulberry tree, and a huge oak graced the grounds. Squirrel boxes and bird houses, constructed by John and son Jerry through the years, hung from the trees.

And as a family at mealtime, mother, father, two daughters and a son, we sat on a screened, later-glass-enclosed back porch and dined. We stared at the sparrows in the birdhouse and they stared back. Bird watchers and people watchers.

Bird families came and went and grew. We saw parent birds send forth their fledglings. Once we watched one mother sparrow pull and tug at a young bird reluctant to

43

leave the nest until it was downright embarrassing. She finally yanked him all the way outside through the round doorway and onto the perch and literally pushed the baby bird with a hard shove. He flapped his wings and flew. Then tried to fly back into the house.

It reminded me of the woman with seven children. When one went away to college, the next child moved up to his room and had a room to himself. One son wanted to return home to stay and his mother told him, "Sorry son, but you lost your place. Stay in the basement if you want to."

John was the motivating force in the overall pervasiveness of nature in our house. He was the calming element (for me, at least). The children seemed to have no repugnance for anything. I gloried in their spunk and freshness and ingenuity, even as I drew back in my overly-female quaverings.

Kitty, our oldest, in the second grade, loved roly-poly bugs, sometimes called sow bugs. I don't know the technical name for them. They are opaquely black, and roll into a tiny ball if you touch them. Unknown to me, she had one in a small match box and carried it to school with her. She came home one afternoon and exclaimed in rapturous tones:

"Mama, guess what? My roly-poly had babies. I poured the roly-poly out on my desk at school today, and there were all those roly-poly babies."

She was exuberant. I was stunned into silence.

John was always bringing things home to the children or me. One day he arrived home from out of town with a gopher turtle, or tortoise, a land turtle. He'd found it on a country road. He and Jerry, about ten at the time, built a gopher or tortoise pen at the back corner of the yard. Jerry delighted in feeding lettuce and apple peelings to the new pet. He had worked his way up and down the ladder of bugs and wormy-type things through the years.

Our youngest daughter was fascinated by frogs and chameleons. She once wrote a great poem about a chameleon. And she used to sit on the backyard sidewalk at night beneath the umbrella of wisteria that John had so patiently trained to that shape. Our daughter would study the toads that hopped there every night near the birdbath. She became proficient enough to paint several vibrating pictures of vivid bright-eyed huge green frogs that, to this day, smile froggily at me from my study walls, to my treasured delight. Some days I raise my eyes and smile froggily back.

Those years with nature include me, one Saturday morning, trying to hang laundered clothes on a line while bees kept buzzing all around me in the air. And John kept saying, "Stand still. They won't hurt you. Just stand still."

"Not me," I called as I ran toward the house and safety. "They think I am a daisy."

Some things are forever impressed on me from the years in that house, our large-gardened small home.

Once I wrote to my mother years and years ago of my husband and children:

In their father, they have a strengthening and refreshing person living in concepts of Christ's teaching.

And again, over twenty years ago, when our children were little I wrote in a letter:

We have had our gas turned off, and have moved the eating headquarters to the back porch. It's wonderful here, with the twittering of the birds, the combined fragrances of red roses on the trellis, the white hedge flowers in bloom, and the whole back fence of yellow honeysuckle.

The mulberry tree is a mass of shade. And sagging with the weight of mulberries, and ours and neighborhood kids clambering all over and up into it, picking and eating the berries. Every kid's mouth and teeth are deep purple.

Yellow and red lilies are in bloom. Red, lavender, pink and white mixed verbena are solid blossoms. And white shastas and yellow black-eyed susans are ready to break open.

There are so many things we think we need. But when you can sit on your back porch and witness so much God-made grandeur, there isn't a thing more we need.

Except perhaps a soul large enough, with the capacity to drink in and saturate our minds with the beauty of it all. To comprehend and be thankful for the privilege of having it here at our fingertips.

* * *

One happening that seared me emotionally, while we lived in that small home, was watching the manner in which our oldest daughter, Kitty, aged ten, dealt with the death, in a distant city, of an aunt she loved dearly.

We learned that Saturday morning of the death of Helen, the young wife of my husband's youngest brother. They had lived in Mobile awhile before moving away. Helen and Kitty had become enduringly close. It was hard to have to tell our ten-year-old that her Aunt Helen had died.

She looked at us with her huge brown eyes and did not say a word. She went out into the yard, walking slowly. She wandered about and then she began to gather flowers that were in bloom. White snowdrops, golden jonquils, yellow jasmine, violets from her own little flower

46

bed, and a neighbor's fallen camellia japonica blossoms of deep pinks and reds which she'd been given permission to have anytime she wished.

She went into the house and took a coat hanger from a closet. Then she asked her Daddy for his wire cutters from his workshop out back. "I need them," she said simply.

In the back yard she snipped at the coat hanger and fashioned a circle of it. Then, interspersing the greenery of the flowing yellow jasmine tapers, she wove her flowers into a wreath.

She took the wreath into the kitchen, opened the refrigerator door and placed the wreath on a shelf. She looked at me solemnly as I stood there at the stove, then turned and walked forlornly out. I could not ask her then because my eyes were brimming with tears, but later when I had control of myself, I asked her what she was going to do with the wreath.

"I don't know," she said. "Let Daddy take it to Birmingham, I guess."

The funeral was to be in Birmingham. John would go alone. Complications with the children, one still a small baby, prevented my going.

Every time I opened the refrigerator door and saw the wreath lying there, I started crying.

When John was ready to leave, Kitty wrapped her wreath in wax paper and put it in the back of the car. John said later that a few of the flowers were wilted when he got there, but many were still fresh. The fresh ones were woven into some of the floral offerings at the foot of Helen's casket. In my heart I felt that Helen knew of the gift of love.

I had about gotten over the emotional effect of Kitty's

wreath when Monday afternoon, John, in his always thoughtful way, brought Jerry and Kitty some little wild johnny-jump-up plants from the woods, for their flower beds. Each had a flower bed all his own.

Kitty was listening to a favorite radio program and said, "Mama, would you set mine out for me, please?"

I loved working with plants and flowers, so I went out to do it.

I noted with surprise that there was a wooden cross composed of two small slats nailed together and stuck in the center of her garden. But I did not examine it closely. I went ahead and set out the johnny-jump-up plants next to her violet plants which were already showing tiny new buds among the heart-shaped leaves.

And then, as I stooped there on my knees, feeling the rich dark earth beneath my fingers, I saw it. The small white cardboard tag. It was attached with wire to the little cross. And I read the words that our ten-year-old daughter had printed in heavy black pencil: THIS GARDEN IS TO AUNT HELEN.

Nature. God. Love.

How we view and feel, and make known our love. Sometimes quietly. Without spoken words. Sometimes volubly, spilling over with what cannot be self-contained.

For nature helps us to grieve as well as to rejoice.

* * *

And recall how, all through our children's growing-up years, I talked. Oh, how I talked. And over-talked.

Once, when Kitty was fifteen, she tagged me accurately. I was on a word harangue, saying more than needed to be said on any subject. And she suddenly laughed and said, "Mother, you are going to be so happy when you get to heaven."

48

"Kitty," I said, "what do you mean?"

She laughed. "You are going to make a perfect harpist."

And then we both broke up, with hilarious laughter. It was the truth. I always talked too much. But this was good. She could tell me that I did. And we could both laugh about it. There was understanding on her part, and that eternal vow in my heart. *Don't talk so much.*

Even those marvelous college students I worked with for four years at First Baptist Church in Mobile had been tolerant and understanding of me. One of the college girls once put her arms about my shoulders and grinned and said,

"Mrs. Greer, we love you. And for Christmas, we're getting you a soapbox."

But, thank goodness, John balanced me at home. He was strong, the doer, and not too talkative. We were each our own self, individual, and complementing each other.

And so, my heart has that feeling of completeness with my husband, which our son Jerry expressed. I see him, standing there, that fourteen-year-old, beneath the canopy of splendid lavender, sweet-smelling wisteria. We were talking about "nature things." And I, for the thousandth time in my children's lives said,

"You know, you all are so lucky to have a father who could teach you all the wonders of nature, so much knowledge to share with you about these things that I just plain don't know about."

And our son, who usually was a grinning Cheshire, twinkling and boundless with sparkling fun, looked at me with solemn face and said:

49

"Mother, Daddy has taught us the wonderful things about nature. You have helped us see God in them."

* * *

And now, our children were all grown. And here we were. John and I in our own woods. Happy and incredulous. With nature, God, love.

And those animals.

John brought me half a dozen collard plants at my request to put in my beyond-the-kitchen flower bed. He twine-string outlined the bed and I set the collards out, looking forward to the day when I would cook and serve fresh greens that *I* had grown.

I had not counted on our friends the cottontails. The twine went first. Nibbled, clipped, fallen. Then successively, all the six plants.

I could hear the rabbits telling their friends, "Those nice people. Planted those juicy young collard plants just for us." Those nice people. We, the intruders. John said, "Well, they have to eat, too."

It was amazing how people would visit us and marvel at the rabbits, raccoons and other animals. And then tell us how to "catch" the animals. And how we ought to clear the woodlands. And shoot the rabbits. And those beautiful squirrels.

We were always aghast. To us, those marvelous woods were a natural preserve. And whatever resided therein had a right to be.

(Later, John would fence his own garden from the rabbits.)

I beheld a sight one mid-morning and gasped. Pine needles were being shoved forward with a fierce mysteriousness, there at the crest of the upper hillside beyond

50

the yard swing which overlooked the massive lowland and meandering brook.

I could hardly wait for John to get home to tell him about it. Rave is more the word, than tell.

"It was an armadillo," I said excitedly. "You wouldn't believe how huge it was. Enormous. And it looked exactly like a bulldozer shoving those mounds of pine needles with its nose. I thought spooks were shoving those pine needles until I saw the armadillo coming up behind."

John said, "Then that's what has built into the side of the hill." There was a large hole dug into the creek-bank side of the hill, but he had not figured what animal had done it. We felt it was too close to the house for the raccoons.

At night, John and I viewed television in the family room with the double glass door drapes open so we could watch for the night animals. One night a wet-looking, tiny green tree frog leaped up and plastered himself against the glass door.

I said, "He wants to watch TV with us." John said, "His TV snacks will be gnats and mosquitoes while he's watching. He's a helper."

I began collecting bugs, butterflies, moths, picking up little deceased beings (victims of pesticide-treated-ground before the house was built, no doubt). Rhinocerous beetles, locust shells, pale blue bird eggshells, a lizard skeleton, a tiny ossified-like green tree frog, exotic large insects I could not identify. Anything I'd find as I walked in the woods.

John brought me a shed snakeskin one day that he had found in the pumphouse. Soon I had enough specimens to fill a bulletin board. And kept getting more. One day a little girl, distant neighbor, rang my doorbell, smiled at me and said:

"I've brought you this for your collection, Mrs. Greer. I found it in the woods."

It was half a turtle shell. Together she and I sat and searched its origin in the book. It turned out to have been a box turtle. Later she returned and brought a friend.

"Mary wants to see your collection, too," she said. So we all three oohed and aahed.

* * *

I hugged closely to me the memories of all that nature and love through the years in our small home in the city.

But now, I was living in the woods.

And I lived joyfully. In the present.

DON'T WAIT TOO LONG

BEDAZZLING WILD SWEET potato blooms spread all around the edges of the forest surrounding the house where we now lived in the woods. They resembled giant white morning glories with purple hallways.

Some were reclining in the sandy dirt. Others twined about seedling trees: a young oak's thin trunk, circled about by the silken blossoms, a tall frail sassafras, hugged and adorned by the embracing beauties.

I wanted to go outside, commune with them. But I was busy inside the house. Too busy to go outside.

Suddenly, I remembered. Remembered that other time, in that other house. One spring.

All week long I had intended to go outside into the waiting springtime. I kept saying to myself, "I'll get all the chores done, dishes washed, beds made, clothes into suds a-washing, and *then* I will walk into that waiting springtime."

I would sit in the oak yard-swing, feel that outdoor gentleness touch and brush me. *Then,* I would really sit and see and become a part of it.

But not quite yet.

The flamboyant azaleas across the driveway had beckoned me from my kitchen window. Their pinks and lavenders and purples reached eagerly for me. They knew I was looking at them superficially, in deliberate detachment. Their faint, teasing fragrance, present, yet not quite present, wafted over to me.

"Come. You cannot put us off. Come now. Take your hands from the dishwater. Leave those dishes. Beds can wait. When you have a clothes drier, you can wash clothes just as easily at night. . . ."

The pull was so powerful. I almost went out. But I didn't.

I gave in to that part of us that says, "I'll do it later. Tomorrow. After awhile. Anytime but now."

I turned from the window. To the, not dreary, but unending tasks that all wives have performed as their contribution to those they love. Love tasks, I call them. Done by wives, mothers, since Eve cared for Adam, then Cain and Abel.

All day I worked. First one thing, then another. When late evening settled in, I realized in dismay that I had not gone out and become a part of that which so lovingly had offered itself to me—had requested so little, just a moment of my time to share.

All day long I had felt the pull, the gentle magnetism. Once through a window I saw the tranquil white snowdrops with their deep green stems and their tall angular leaves, the graceful drops of white, hanging face down from dainty curving throats.

Above them splashed mountainfalls of azaleas so deeply purple-pink they took on a literal phosphorescence. In the quietest majesty imaginable, they begged me to come out.

"Tomorrow morning, for sure. Right after breakfast, I'll walk out on all this work. Go and be a part of all that splendor that God sends, which we call Spring."

That's what I told myself.

But in the night, the rains came. Hard rains. The kind of rain that bears welcome water for roots deep in the ground to send nourishment up through marvelous networks of nature, that results in what we call, so simplistically, leaves and blooms.

The kind of rain that also, alas, assaults. Beats down, and calls to an end the peak of effulgent splendor of poetry in petals that have reigned, abundant and regal, in tender and delicate glory.

This was the morning I would go out, hold hands with the beauty; love and be loved by the springtime floral grandeur.

"You waited too long." No accusation in the beaten blossoms. A simple statement, sent to me on bruised and sodden flowers.

I was smitten suddenly by all the times I had waited too long.

"Mama, come look at the redbird."

"Just a minute, Honey, let me finish sweeping the floor."

"Oh, Mama. It's gone. The redbird's gone."

Too long. Just a moment. That could have been snatched and grabbed from nothing that could not be interrupted. Nothing that wouldn't have waited and still been there, to be completed later.

The sudden immersion in awareness, and remorse, went deep inside me. It pained me. I sighed softly and vowed that I would remember long after the moment. That not only would I remember, but that I would remember with response, with proper placement of values.

And so it was, these many years later, living in the

woods, our children all grown and gone, that on this evening after John was home from work and we had finished our supper, there was still some daylight lingering, touching the woods with pink quilted wonder.

And John said:

"Let's go walking in the woods, and down by the creek."

"I've got to do these dishes," I said.

Something on his face, some little trace of . . . what was it . . . stabbed me. . . .

Memory of the long ago fallen and bruised, pink and purple blossoms . . . of that unrecoverable little child's voice in its throb of unspoken, you-didn't-love-me-enough-to-come-when-I-wanted-to-share-with-you, and the spoken, "It's gone, Mama. The redbird's gone."

I smiled at my husband. That pink quilted twilight wouldn't wait for anyone.

"Let's go. These dishes can wait."

A LETTER OR TWO

June 1

Dear Sister Dot,

The offer still holds if you need me during or after your gall bladder operation.

One other thing, since I'm a know-it-all. When you undergo a general anesthetic, it takes a lot out of you. So be prepared to feel under-par for a long while in getting your strength back.

I had minor surgery several years ago (I was a hospital volunteer, then). I figured I would be up and back at the volunteer work within a week.

I was shaken to find that it took me almost three months to get my plain old strength back. So a major *operation takes a long time to get over.*

Now that I've told you things you doubtless already know . . . on to other things.

My raccoon came back! I was so overjoyed that he wasn't the one mowed to death by the automobile.

The raccoon and possum are regular night callers at our back doorsteps. We put out food for them, biscuits, bread, sometimes meat. Next morning, everything is licked clean. We watch them from the door or window sometimes.

One night we forgot to put out food for them. So, to protest our neglect the raccoon (a possum couldn't have managed it)

57

turned over the garbage can, pulled the lid off. I can just see him huffing and puffing in indignation, and tugging at that lid like a human. He strewed garbage all the way from the over-turned can clear up into the upper woods.

Christie and I spent almost one whole day trying to organize and categorize the books in my study. I told John one day, as he was moving a pile of lumber,

"You've spent most of your life moving piles of lumber and I've spent most of my life moving stacks of books."

But with all the plunder each of us has accumulated, we've seldom been guilty of that incriminating and devastating accu-sation, "What in the world are you saving that *for?"*

If you save something for ten or twenty years and never need it, then finally, in a monumental heroism, discard it reluc-tantly, two days after the garbage man hauls it away, you have a sudden unprecedented imperative for that item, and that item alone. I am reading Candide. *And Thurber and Leacock. And* Job for Modern Man, Tried and True *by American Bible Society. What are you reading?*

* * *

Dear Sweet Daughter Kitty,
This complete changeover of a life pace has taken a long while.

Yet finally it was accomplished. At long last, as you might say, we have blended into the woodwork and the woods.

No aftermath in the true sense of the word set in. But for me, there were little twinges. Not of a looking back, or yearning, exactly. But a temporary sort of displaced feeling hovered about, settled in on me for several weeks after we moved into the house.

It was strange. How do truly displaced people, those humans in that true agony of ruptured displacement, blasted without warning into a chaos of nowhere to call their own, no place to

58

orient their being . . . how do they survive it?

Yet all around, from that hell of Hitler's era, to Vietnam, to the awful daily complacent carnage on our concrete ribbons of highways which we traverse like frenzied ants . . . people pick themselves up and reside in displacement. So my feelings (enormous in small moments) weren't even fringes of the real excruciation of displacement.

From out of all this, there must come something.

I recall that Beatrix Potter had no little friends as a child, her bedroom had bars on the windows, she had a dour governess. But she was allowed to have a pet rabbit. Ergo, The Tales of Peter Rabbit. *Classic forever.*

Write about what you know, they say . . . and the world is blest.

What could I do with a raccoon, a possum, a blue-tailed skink (look it up), a rabbit, an armadillo, six squirrels, all those birds and a couple of snakes.

Where we really live, in the kitchen, in the family room, and in the bedroom, big double windows or glass doors face out onto the remarkable rain forest of vast bay trees, brooding magnolias, slim wild cherry, oaks and pines, blackgums, yellowtulip poplars and other trees we are occasionally just discovering and identifying.

Moving up and all among those tree giants, are those unworldly Tarzan-like scuppernong vines hanging there, sometimes moved by the wind, or birds, or squirrels, but always there with an additional solidity uniquely theirs. And the animals, the creatures, the creepers and crawlers. . . .

We have a raccoon and possum as nightly visitors to our backdoor. Squirrels and rabbits feed at dawn and dusk, in the same feeding area outside the kitchen double windows. We see tracks of an armadillo being chased by dogs into the swamp.

And of course, that entrancing little stream, gently flowing

59

water that courses its weaving little way through our woods. Daddy has cleared three small clearings alongside the stream. We sit and know what it is to be in the forest primeval.

Uncle Jim and Aunt Joyce came over one Sunday recently. Jim barbecued ribs on the patio grill. He loves to barbecue. They come over almost every week. We live so much nearer to each other now.

Uncle Jim is in pain most of the time, suffers almost constant feeling of nausea, but is still working, full five days a week.

The word cancer *has never been said. He knows they took out his gall bladder and "did something to my stomach." But he makes an occasional reference to the future as though his is not as long as everyone else's.*

He doesn't talk of it, nor dwell on it. He keeps avoiding the hardest . . . and seems to be following the path that Granddaddy did, who had the same thing.

Kitty, I will keep all your little memorabilia until you want us to send it. It isn't such a large lot, but somehow because it was yours and a part of you, I couldn't bring myself to discard any of it.

Little keepsakes from one's childhood, not enormously significant, but a tiny ribbon linking us with our distant beginnings.

We're supposed to get a telephone, quote middle of June unquote. From April 7 to middle of June is a long time way out here in these woods.

I'll hasten, jog and sprint down the circular dirt driveway down to the outer red-dirt drive across our moat (swamp) to the mailbox and put up the little red flag on our mailbox. I'm trying hard each time to remember that little red flag.

MORE LETTERS

I KNOW that God is found not only in isolation, but in contact with God's human creatures as well. And yet, the woods bring me close to Him. And I feel His presence so intensely in the woods that I seem caught up in the *unfolding* of the Divine before my very eyes.

So many feelings come to me. And who can ever totally account for the depths of feelings.

I had the strangest sensation one morning in June, the tenth, I think it was. This feeling came over me that the last portion of my life was opening into a vastness that I never dreamed of. I just knew that I was walking forward, that waters were parting wide into a path leading where I did not know. But leading.

It was a strange sensation. Mysticism. Maybe. Faith. Surely. I could not explain what prompted it. I merely sat in the woods and knew it. I felt it with my whole being, almost as if God had touched me lightly on the shoulder. Many times I have been very quiet, and felt God's presence. This time it was different. And very strange. As if an overwhelming outpouring of His love had reached out for me and held me close.

Dear Sweet Mother,

There are a couple of little lively blue-tailed skinks (striped lizards) who skitter alongside in the leaves as I walk down the driveway leading to the mailbox.

Instead of scurrying away from me, they almost accompany me down the edge of the underbrush. Nature-things are peculiar, aren't they? No more so than humans, which I suppose are also nature-things.

I went back to Sunday School and church last Sunday morning. It is thirty miles there and back from these woods.

We had disbanded the college evening group temporarily several months ago. I am not certain the college group will be reorganized as such. I am not certain that I will even keep going. That is a long distance to travel to church. I keep wondering if I should find a smaller church out this way and try to get active with young people again. We've called a new minister to our church now that our minister of the past twenty-five years has retired.

I had a letter from our mutual friend. His beliefs in his new religion are quite strong, as I made them out. I found more adamance than clarity, or even charity.

Ironbound, unyielding inflexibility in religious fervor may bring joy to the wielder, but not always to those it is being wielded against. I find religious discussions interesting and revealing. But I do not participate in them for long unless I feel that pathways to understanding are truly being opened.

It is amazing to me sometimes, how spiritual feelings can be imparted to others when God or Jesus aren't mentioned by name. What love for others I learned, I learned from you. By your being, *not by your preaching. I learned love from you. We all did.*

I sit frequently down in Dogwood Bower beside the talking creek. It is so other-worldly, secluded, overhung with low dog-

wood and towering poplars. We have folding chairs and tables and benches there. Bruiser and I sit for hours. I take lunch down there and read and write.

The waters are so like music and throb in my ears (I all but sit in the water, I get that close). Someone could cart off the house and I'd never hear it. It is heavenly in the bottomland.

* * *

Dear Son Jerry,

We, the house, the territory and the animals are all fine. Bruiser has found some female somewhere in these hills and he is more absent than with us. He comes dragging in, his tongue hanging down an inch above the ground after running all day with the country-side BIG dogs. He forgets, that by human standards, he is a ninety-five-year-old dog!

Daddy looks wonderful. Gets handsomer as the years roll on. His health is fine.

It is still a marvelous pleasure living in this house in these woods.

Uncle Jim is doing very poorly. We go over several times a week. I take him desserts. Sometimes he can keep it down, sometimes not. But he loves sweets, and seems so genuinely pleased when we come in bringing him something.

Aunt Joyce says he gets up in the morning, puts his clothes on, then has to spend most of the time lying down. His stomach hurts all the time. It tears us up to see him.

JULY

THE MONTH of July leapfrogged with lightning across the summer sky. I stayed indoors most of the time in the cool of air-conditioning. The hot humid outdoors did not beckon me.

Except in early mornings. John and I sat on the patio before breakfast and drank coffee. Still not believing the woodland beauty all around us. We saw the faint sun touching into the forest about us. And marveled at the prisms, the glintings. A spiderweb spreading across the lowland walkway showed itself suddenly, revealed by sun-glistened threads.

And early evenings, we did the same. Drank coffee on the patio. And felt the day wind itself downward into night. Fireflies, frogs, the whirring of an owl. And always in my mind, I could hear that clear strident call, the whippoorwill.

It was not there, except in my mind. It was long gone. I hoped it would return next year.

And something else we heard. And could hardly believe, such beauty. Neither of us had known it before.

We *heard* it first, this flute-like caroling, spilling and filling the woods with such music we were breathless. But we could never see the bird, nor trace the source of the harmonics.

Then one day, I saw two beige and brown speckled birds feeding on the grain just beyond the kitchen patio.

I hurried to the "book." I found a picture in color. And the maker of melody was spelled out in descriptive words there on a page.

There was no doubt. That's what our untroubled trilling troubadour on a tall tall tree in the deep deep forest was. A woodthrush.

Throughout the day there were redbirds, towhees, redbellied woodpeckers, blackbirds with gleaming yellow eyes, blue jays, and one day I saw a pileated woodpecker . . . twittering, chirping, peeping, squawking, squeaking. Feeding at the kitchen windows at back, and at the front driveway where we placed grain morning and night.

And also feeding at the grain places, day and night, mixing incongruously with the birds, were a dozen squirrels cavorting, and a solemn-eyed rabbit, shortly to be three rabbits. The heterogeneity of the strange amalgam of critters was amazing. They would scamper into the wood's edge at our approach, but would never go far away.

The possum and raccoon came nightly. We'd watch them. They would watch us. Separated only by windowed walls.

One night while the raccoon was eating on the shelf where we placed food for them between two slender trees outside the kitchen, the possum came up. He met the eyes of the raccoon, then turned and took off.

First time we'd seen them together. Each night by

9:30, one or the other had gotten the food. We'd never seen them there at the same time.

As time would go on, the raccoon became five rac-coons, and one would come openly in the daytime. Up on the patio and peer in the window. It was a signal to me that he (it turned out to be a she, later with young ones) was ready to sup.

I'd go to the door. The raccoon would scamper into the woods, wait until I'd loaded the shelf. A few minutes later, there would be a raccoon, up on the shelf, eating away.

I would open the family room sliding glass door and talk to her through the screen door. It intoxicated me that she tolerated me this much.

One Saturday morning, John called to me. "Come down here, I want you to see something."

He had discovered a huge snapping turtle about two feet long in the creek. Enormous and covered with green moss. It looked like some prehistoric creature to me.

We would see other turtles, on land, and in the creek. One which John called me to see, turned out to be a "map turtle." So-called because its shell markings actu-ally resemble a road map.

He pulled it out of the water and discovered its head was covered with leeches. John tried to scrape them off with a stick to relieve the turtle. To no avail. The leeches were the ugliest things I have ever seen.

They clung, like slimy, working, affixed maggots to the map turtle's head. John was unable to budge them. They were leeches in the clinging blood-sucking classic sense of the term. If leeches could be called classic.

He slipped the turtle back into the small stream to

fight its natural enemy in its own way. Or succumb. Which ever it would be.

The floors of the woodlands held their own embroidery and appliqué handworks of beauty—the wild hibiscus the color of soda biscuits, wild lavender sweet peas, twined around a lanky, lacy weed, proud prim dwarf sunflowers, a nest of morning glories, purple-throated beauties, blooming in a washed out rut where the earlier rains had cut.

Mountain laurel on the high embankments had relinquished their early reign of pink complex beauty. Now the swamp azaleas, pale pink, quietly preened.

Turquoise-imprinted dragonflies thrummed exotically in the lowlands, helicoptering over the brook and fernery. Pale purple groundmoths were nervously hyperactive. Monarch butterflies flitted, angular, elegant.

In the outer swamp by the road-edge, cattails spired tall among their flat greenery, like browned weiners. The high-branched leaves of cerise maples and yellow poplars fluttered and giggled at the caresses of stray movements of air. Squirrels leaped happily throughout the woods when not at their front or backyard cracked-corn feeding places.

* * *

Intermittently, we visited Jim and Joyce in the evenings. Jim looked terrible and felt awful. His color was ashen-green. With his clothes on, lying in the bed, he would always get up and sit in a chair when we arrived. His eyes would drift open and then close. But he engaged in whatever conversation was going on.

It was a far more ill Jim than the one with whom I'd had a conversation the week before I went to Atlanta.

67

We'd gone to visit them on a Saturday afternoon. Joyce was showing John some of her beautiful plants out in the yard. Jim and I were sitting in their den.

Somehow the conversation came around to God.

Jim said, "You know, I never have been much of one to go to church. But I believe in God, and Jesus. I don't do much talking about it, but I believe."

"I know you do, Jim," I said. "Your life shows it, the way you treat people and the way you live in relation to others."

At the time of this conversation, I remembered another talk Jim and I had had almost two years before. On the telephone, long before our move to the woods.

He had called to find out how we were. I answered, and talked with him before calling John to the phone.

I told Jim, "I'm trying to work on a speech for a church group, about some summer missionary work our college young people have done with a remedial reading program for underprivileged children in an inner city mission."

I said, "Sometimes I wonder who I am to be telling others how to live Christian lives. I feel I have a lot of nerve."

He gave me what I needed at the moment, a word of encouragement.

"More of us ought to be standing up, having the courage to speak up," he said. "You're doing the right thing."

I thought of these things as we visited in his home and saw this man, my husband's brother, in his suffering.

And he was so pleased when we came to visit. His face would light with joy.

68

Then on July 30, Jim went into the hospital. He was almost dehydrated.

It was a threshold for Jim and his family.

And for me, it was a doorway I had not anticipated.

AUGUST

THREE SOUNDS resembled each other deep in the woods. Distant thunder. A Whisperjet taking off from the airport two miles away. And a downhill dump truck thumping over the road in the valley half a mile from us before it began its climb to the next crest. Inside our well-insulated house, the three sounds in inception were indistinguishable one from the other.

Down in the canopied glen of Dogwood Bower, the sounds of cars out on the busy road—cars hidden from view by the woodlands—roared past, people going to town, to work, to school.

But another sound was more immediate. That ceaseless murmur of the stream that gossiped lispingly over worn-smooth jutting brown tree roots.

I sat silent beside it. The brook, the green ferns, the mouldering water-fallen log lavished with green moss, lichen, mushrooms and scuppernong roots; the stumpy behemoth of a half bay tree (its top, the mouldering log felled by some great storm) rising stolid like an elephant's hind leg stuck there occupying half the stream.

Part of the musical sound was the brook's waters passing noisily around the bay trunk's elephant-like foot in a small passageway, and stirring up a small curvature of foamy spit in a tiny rooty bay.

A truck roared by in the distance, and a small plane buzzed overhead like a June bug.

The air in that secluded place was dank and heady. Scuppernong vines, green and covering, reached in all directions. Fallen brown pine needles clung to leaves and branches of trees and bushes, dangling like beaded curtains.

To look upward, was to be overwhelmed by the incredible height of bay trees, tulip-poplars and pines and maple and wild cherry, blackgum and sourwood. Just overhead were the low dogwoods and maples that fashioned the bower-seclusion which drew me so often into this away-from-the-world place.

To sit. And feel. Sometimes to think. But mostly to feel and blend.

I would just sit and know the sounds. Birds twittering, peeping, chirping, squeaking. A scurrying sound turned into a huge solemn-faced rabbit who jumped the brook, came stirring 'round a bend in the underbrush, stopped motionless when he saw me (in *his* bower, no doubt), whirled and took off, back to wherever he came from.

Sounds and sights and smells impinged upon me, moved into me, becoming one with me. A sunshine yellow poplar petal fell in languid spiral. That leaf was I. I fell languidly, lazily, then spun dizzily on the rushing little waters on my way to the Mobile Bay, or to be caught up against a craggy root, pushed into a corner, to vegetate, moulder, dwindle, disintegrate and become a part of the whole once more. The whole to which we all belong.

I would sit and blend. At other times, something would trigger me. The suspenseful watching of a wild flower in its unfolding, waiting for the buds to open—tantalized day by day, wondering what form the flowers would take, what color the blossoms.

Then a force would attack my brain, mechanize it, and urge, force me to try to share what I was now a part of. The agony was that like love—it was indefinable, incommunicable. One must experience it himself.

Why did I keep wanting to define it, keep wanting to give to someone else glimpses of it through my eyes.

Every person is where he is. I kept wanting to say: this is where I am.

I was thinking over and over, in wanting to share it: this is where I am. Wherever you are, I hope all is well with you. It was as if I wanted to shout to the world, enjoy, love, be glad, and I wish that you could share this glorious place with me.

I had gone into the lowland dogwood nook at 7:30 A.M. By 9 A.M. the eastern sky, which had spilled sunshine throughout the woods, was now clouding over. After awhile when I would go back into the house, I would hear faint rumbles. I would not know at first whether it was thunder, a jet plane, or a dump truck.

* * *

We visited Jim in the hospital almost daily, or nightly, after John came home from work. Jim, sallow and gaunt, was now retaining his food, able to eat. Permission had been gained from his doctor for us to bring him the desserts which he liked. "Anything he wants," the doctor had said.

For a few days I returned to my volunteer work at

Mobile General Hospital, working Visitor Control and substituting at other services.

I had not definitely returned regularly to church and Sunday School. The fifteen mile drive deterred me mentally. And I was not serving as a leader or teacher. Subconsciously, I was still trying to decide whether to find a smaller nearer church and attend it, or to return conclusively to downtown First Baptist Church of Mobile. Fifteen miles each way seemed so much more than that former three miles from our other house. As, indeed it was.

After a week of hospital volunteer work, I bowed out because Joyce needed me occasionally for transportation to Mobile Infirmary. She and their two sons and their wives scheduled themselves to stay with Jim at all times.

When I went outdoors to sit in the woods, I left a window open. I remained in hearing distance of the telephone.

One night when we were visiting Jim, he said suddenly, "I like Mobile. I might die before I get to see all I want to."

He began coughing. His skin was increasingly yellowed and he was weaker. His bright vivid brown eyes stared in a dilated way.

By mid-August he was sleeping fitfully most of the time between pain shots. He would talk ramblingly, then catch himself.

Intermittently, with eyes glazed, he spoke in monologues which began abruptly and ceased abruptly . . .

"I know I saw somebody wearing a purple dress . . . I've got to find them . . . that automobile down on the corner has to have a mechanic . . . and those painters aren't doing those walls right. . . ."

Under the medication these incidents seemed real to him. His brow furrowed and he was in that misery of semi-stupor. He spoke whatever his mind snared.

Then he would catch himself and say to Joyce, "Honey, I'm crazy . . . I'm dreaming again. . . ."

Joyce would smile. She had lived so much with the wasting away of the man she loved, the mere smiling at the extreme monologues served as a tension reliever for her.

But it was a quickly-gone smile. Joyce and I talked about this "rambling" of the mind that is drugged, but not quite into unconsciousness.

We were sitting across coffee cups in the hospital cafeteria. We took the break to give her a momentary respite from the almost unbearable time in the sick room. Hours in a sick room are longer than those ticked off by the clock.

"It is the same with everyone of us. If you take any given morning, alone at home in our kitchen, going about our work. From one task to another, our mind hops and jumps, starts off in one direction, then leaps onto another track. It's hard to know how one ever gets to any particular thought," I said.

She said, "We'd sound just like he does if we said it out loud . . . he's saying it out loud."

We could see Jim's struggle in his mind trying to surface with the words . . . at the split moment he *was* his words.

* * *

During this time of Jim's illness, one night I noticed a small bulge on my right rib-area as I stepped out of the

74

shower. I stood before the walled mirror in my dressing room, drying off.

I barely thought about it at the time. I didn't even stare at it, just noticed it in passing as I wrapped the towel about me and dried my dripping body.

A strange bird showed up at breakfast the next morning. Dazzling yellow, very small, black mask over his face, underside all yellow, and yellow legs and feet. He flew in following a red bird, to the cracked corn-millet feeding area beyond the kitchen windows. I saw him later in the dogwood branches outside my study window.

"Maybe he'll tarry," I thought. I couldn't identify him.

We continued to visit Jim, and take the desserts.

Joyce told me once, "Last night at midnight, Jim ate the Jello-cake with whipped topping you brought him. The nurse had kept it in the refrigerator for him. He hadn't had a bite to eat of anything since breakfast."

She laughed and added, "Jim said, 'Virginia didn't use to cook this well!' "

Another of my husband's sisters-in-law came down from Birmingham to stay with Joyce and to help around the clock with Jim.

By the last week in August, Jim was weaker, cogent only in brief periods. I went in to the hospital during the middle of the day. The weather was intensely August, suffocatingly hot. In the western sky, rumbles and conglomerates of dark clouds boded thunderstorm.

Jim was sitting on the side of the bed, feet hanging over, his food tray across his midriff. He held a fork in his hand. He greeted me with a wan smile, then returned to that in-and-out awareness.

He lifted his fork halfway to his mouth, then dozed. Joyce guided his hand to his mouth. He opened his eyes, smiled sheepishly and opened his mouth, took a bite of potato and began to chew.

An accumulation of fluid had to be drained one day. Then he had a spell of bleeding, which was stopped. He was now sleeping in long stretches, not talking except vaguely, recognizing various people present when he roused.

Now, two people had to stay with him. He would struggle upward with a violent unheralded strength. He would get out of bed before anyone could hold him down.

John and I went into town to the hospital the evening of August 29. Jim was in a semi-coma, his face sunken, eyes far back in his face, skin pale and yellow.

As we walked down the corridor to leave at the close of visitors' hours, a friend of ours, a licensed practical nurse, came hurrying down the hall to greet us. We embraced, she and I. We were longtime dear friends. And as we did, on impulse, I said,

"Feel this. What do you think?"

I placed her hand on my rib-side. She could feel the small protuberance through the fabric of my blouse.

Her face was serious. "You'd better get to the doctor. And tomorrow, too. He's leaving town in three days to be gone three weeks." (He was her doctor, too.)

"I guess I can't avoid facing it," I said. "The little place is bothering me."

The rib was aching slightly and a very small swelling was evident. I assumed it was from an old rib sprain I'd sustained over twenty years ago when our youngest daughter was a baby. I'd slipped on a throw rug and fallen on my right ribcage against the side of the letdown baby bed.

The ribs had ached for six months or so, although

believe it or not, I had not gone to the doctor with it. Just sort of suffered it out. And eventually it eased.

And so, now I went to my doctor. He examined me. His face showed no alarm. I explained to him the long-ago rib hurt. "That might be it, but to be safe, we'd better get X-rays made." He gave me a slip to take to the hospital X-ray Department.

I felt no urgency about it. He said in all his long years of practice he'd never seen a malignancy in that spot.

The next day I went to sit with Jim to relieve Joyce and my visiting sister-in-law. On impulse again, when they returned, I said, "I believe while I'm here, I'll go on down to X-ray and get this chest-ray made."

The films were made. I told the technician I wanted to talk to the radiologist who read the film, that my doctor was leaving town two days later. I wanted to know whether I should get in touch with him before I left the hospital. (I was not always within reach of the phone, being at the hospital with Jim and Joyce some of the time. The doctor might not be able to get in touch with me.)

The radiologist walked up to me. "Your doctor may want to make further tests."

"Further tests?" I said. "What do you mean, what kind of tests?"

He said, "Well, he might want a biopsy."

Somehow his saying that seemed foolish to me. There was nothing to "bi-op" as far as I was concerned. You couldn't call that little swelling beneath my rib a lump to biop. It was just a little swelling.

Another thunderstorm broke wildly and violently during the afternoon before I went home. That night John went in to stay with Jim.

Sassafras mittens were turning red and the sourwood

trees were beginning to color. Squirrels hopped and leaped in branches, almost flying from tree to tree high in the pines and oaks. And the blackgums were taking on Christmas colors in August.

The woods were still God's wonders to me. And I saw the many little wild flowers there to please the eye.

"Would that we humans could be as pleasing to each other," I thought as I sat out in the swing beneath the pines and oaks. Each morning I seemed to redeem from the outdoors everything made for the soul.

My doctor called that evening to ask me how my pain was.

"It's not really a pain," I said. "More like a small ache." He wanted me to see his partner later for a full report of the X-ray film. He and his wife were leaving the next morning.

My sister-in-law called the next day, early. She and a daughter-in-law of Jim's were going in to stay with him. Joyce had been there around the clock and was going home with another daughter-in-law to get some rest.

On September 2, I picked up my visiting-sister-in-law and she and I spent the day with Jim. His breathing was labored.

The next morning, we were called about 5:30 A.M. Jim was worse. We arrived about 8 A.M. and stayed until four P.M. that Sunday. It was painful to watch that incredible struggle put up by Jim to sustain alertness even with pain shots, rest shots, and sleeping pills. A true fight.

Our phone rang at 3:40 A.M. the next morning, Monday, Labor Day. It was my sister-in-law from Birmingham.

Jim was dying.

When John and I arrived, Jim had already gone.

He had struggled, fighting for alertness. He recognized Joyce at the last moment as he said, "Honey."

And with his last breath, a beautiful smile had come upon his face.

SEPTEMBER

BERGSON, in his *Introduction to Metaphysics,* speaks of two ways of knowing a thing. The relative way and the absolute way. The first, by point of view, implying that as we move around the object we gain the knowledge. The second, by intuition, by moving into the object with a kind of intellectual sympathy, by which one places himself within an object in order to coincide with what is unique in it, and consequently inexpressible.

The consoling truth of the immortal spirit came to me slowly.

I sought my being in the being of the woods. Each morning after my husband departed for work, I sat in the chaise lounge at the wood-edge of the upper drive beyond the front of the house. Thinking, reading, sometimes writing.

The early morning was a world I could see and hear as at no other time. Squirrels leaping in their circuitry of the woods. Tree limbs, oaks, pines, sassafras, dogwood, bending to their leaps, then springing back with whispers or crackles or rattles or waggles.

Small birds made sounds like rusty hinges, flitted

among boughs, pecking at berries or bugs. Small sounds of leaves and pine needles. Wildflowers, purple, red-orange, white, pale yellow, and ground-hugging peas, pink, yellow, wind-touched jewels.

Chameleons of deceptive brown, and skinks in natty blue-yellow stripes, darted in all directions surveying staked-out territories, tipping twigs even as pine needles pierced the air.

Flocks of crows winged over, cawing raucously. Mockingbirds sang a capella. Quail, now covied, flared up in wingbeating groups when startled, like a many-engined gawky helicopter.

And what was the sun doing to the sky, suddenly turning it a transcendental blue with early hints of October in a mid-September sky.

Cicadas were filling the air like ham radio operators. Such small insects to make so rampant a sound. Filling and swelling and expanding and amplifying, the sound encompassing and possessing the air. It was deafening.

How different from that earlier springtime clear-encircling evening sound of the whippoorwill. How I missed it. It had been so welcome, come evening, with its total, refined encirclement. It seemed to me such a haunting love offering.

The cicada's cry was an insistent symphony of discordance. Yet it, too, was welcome, as part of the whole. But like an unruly guest, it hogged the conversation and disrupted gentle thought, aching the brain and short-circuiting smoother mind flow.

I thought of that tiny insect, with his transparent wings. Of that thirteen years underground in his nymph condition. And his emergence as an adult after that long underground sleep. To burgeon. And after a few short weeks of life, to die.

No wonder he makes himself known. He is shouting, "I'm here, I'm here. God's creature. Know that I am here. See me. Hear me. Know me. For my brief time."

I was surrounded by forest, trees, wind, distant traffic. House to the rear of me. Surrounded, closed in, embraced and towered over by oaks and pines and dogwoods, blackgum and sassafras.

My eyes drifted from the pages of the book, my Bible, I held, and looked heavenward. What was I feeling, knowing that at last one day I should infinitely be part of it, forevermore a part of it.

And Jim. How was it with Jim? Where had his soul's spirit gone as it departed from his body just two weeks and one day ago? In that unutterable moment of agony —or was it ecstasy—when abruptly the smile appeared and his body lay still.

Those expert people had prepared his remains, cleansed his body, cosmetically altered the ravages of that cancerous liver to his skin, clothed him in fine raiment, and placed him gently for all to view in a quilted box surrounded by hothouse flowers beneath pale rheostated lights.

The remains were ready. But where was the essence? Where *is* the essence? Jim. Where are you? And all the others?

What form? An entity, amorphous, ethereal, transparent, opaque, cloudy, wispy, foggy, or a spirit of existence without form but not void. Anywhere? Everywhere?

I turned to my Bible, to I Corinthians 2:9,10. *"Eye hath not seen, nor ear heard, neither have entered into the heart of man the things which God hath prepared for them that love him. But God hath revealed them unto us by his Spirit: for the Spirit searcheth all things, yea, the deep things of God."* And 15:44: *"There is a natural body, and there is a spiritual body."*

Then in Ecclesiastes 12:7 I found, *"Then shall the dust return to the earth as it was: and the spirit shall return unto God who gave it."*

If I think of you, Jim, you are here, body, feeling, thought, being. Yet not as body do I think of you.

It is as being, as presence, as comforting bridgeway, reaching and touching. For whether you were well, or ill, even bedridden, always it was the being, the vibrating, the communing as family.

And so, we remember the departed. In the communing, the bridging, the touching of spirits when the body was yet alive. But the touching, the communing more important than the flesh.

For the spirit of the body exists before the body departs. And it is the spirit that speaks, both before and after death which is the departure point of the body.

The spirit.

The cicadas screamed. The electric pump in the pumphouse throbbed, harsh and pulsating. I did not need to wonder where one will be after bodily death. I thought of Jesus, our dear Savior, son of God who suffered and died for us all, yet who said gently, *"Peace I leave with you, my peace I give unto you"* (John 14:27).

And there in the woods a great and awesome peace came over me.

83

Later, I went to help Joyce with her sympathy thank-you notes. "I can't bring myself to do it yet," she said. "I want you to do it for me." She asked me to write the personal notes for her.

And as she and I conferred over the notes, I thought, "I am doing this for Joyce. But I am also doing it for Jim." They were so close as husband and wife, I knew that he would be grateful for my help to Joyce.

Then a large feeling (or was it knowledge?) hit me . . . Is this what Jesus meant when he said, *"Tend my sheep"* (John 21:16)? Our love for Christ should make us do for others because they are loved by Christ. They are his "sheep." His loved ones.

"That is Christ out there," I thought. Not only our kin. But those neighbors. And strangers.

"And when I hurt someone, a stranger, a neighbor, a child, a friend, I hurt Christ. . . ."

For Christ, in the parable, said, *"Inasmuch as ye did it not to one of the least of these, ye did it not to me"* (Matthew 25:45).

And I thought in penitence, "When ye did it *not* unto them, ye did it not unto me. . . ."

I prayed, "God help us. Forgive us. Use us. Remind us and strengthen us against our selfish selves.

And let us not forget that Jesus who did love us, loves us yet.

That Jesus who died, lives."

* * *

I had attended Sunday School and church services occasionally the past few weeks. I had listened to the interim pastor. Then there came an invitation in the mail. An invitation to attend the Church Leadership Banquet on September 20, in the Fellowship

Hall of First Baptist Church. Our new pastor would speak.

I fingered the invitation. Looked at it, thought about it. Would I attend? I didn't know. At that particular time I was not literally a leader in the church, having withdrawn temporarily from co-leadership of the college young people's evening group, which had later disbanded.

And I had still not decided whether to continue going to the downtown church or seek a smaller church, not so distant.

Something impelled me finally to attend the Leadership Banquet. It was a conclusive step.

That evening when I found myself amidst the leadership of First Baptist Church, I was stunned into a feeling I'm not sure I ever experienced before.

I felt myself being bombarded by vibrating love from the eyes and faces of people I had known within the church since my children were very small, growing up in the church.

Teachers of my children from tot-hood to teens, men and women who had contributed to my children's lives, consequently who had touched my own. Young men and women whom I had taught in Sunday School as seven-year-olds, now grown, with children of their own.

Men and women in whose groups I had been a member as an adult, people whose joys and sorrows I had shared through the years. And those beautiful college young people.

The sudden glimpsings and smilings and exchanges of love that night spread like a panorama, encompassing the distant years of my past and reaching lovingly into my future. I had no decision to make.

This was my church.

The next morning, I called our minister of education, and told him what had happened to me at the Leadership Banquet, of my sure knowledge that First Baptist Church was "my church."

I could not know how that very act would affect my life deeply within the next few weeks.

* * *

As I sat beneath the trees, a blue jay pecked acorns atop an oak tree. A squirrel bippity-bopped, circumnavigating the fringe of treetops headed toward the sunflower seeds waiting for him at the kitchen patio feeding ground. A redheaded woodpecker tapped at a high dead limb on a mammoth pine nearby.

I sat with pen and notebook in hand. Not writing. Just sitting there, feeling the cavernous self of the deep woods blending into my total self.

Why was this feeling exploding within me, searching for vent between soul and paper.

I thought of artists. What is it with them. Art is magic to me. I don't understand it. I see it, feel it, but how the artist has created it, I cannot fathom.

I had gone to the Providence Hospital Art Gallery opening with my dear friend, Della, at her invitation. I saw the paintings, water colors and oils, and learned what a "pastel" is.

I had yearned openly for the huge oil painting of "The Washerwoman" by a Mobile artist. I had gazed long at those oils and watercolors, flowers, sky and lakes.

I don't know how they do it. I cannot draw a straight,

or even a crooked line. I cannot paint a straight or crooked flower. Not discernibly so.

But, I wondered whether they, the artists, are driven by the same compulsion I feel, so that they must get down on paper what they see.

I must mix and scramble and daub and dibble the words onto a palette, then select and dip into the paints of words and put them onto paper with the tip of my pen. Pushed into the act by a force beyond myself.

Whatever vision or feeling or knowledge or groping there is within me, pushes forth into words even as smoke in a room will push its way through every hidden crevice, crack and unknown aperture, no matter how tiny. The force pushes. And whatever the propellant, the words emerge.

I kept trying to sort it out as I walked in the woods, as I sat by the flowing little stream. I wandered and thought and felt, in the woods, the everlasting woods.

Between 9:30 and 10 A.M., the big sound from the little creatures, the cicadas, would begin. That small beginning rattle that became a giant pervasiveness and filled the ears and became a part of the very sky.

Bright yellow butterflies winged about and touched the pale yellow wild hibiscus blooms lying in the shallow hillsides beyond the kitchen window. Goldenrods graced autumn's morn in fellowship with sassafras red-and-green mittens. Golden threads of scuppernong loomed themselves among the oaks and fingered a spray of wine-colored sourwood leaves.

The squirrels had come and gone in their lofty perambulations. Vivid red blackgum leaves fluttered and fell.

Falling leaves taking the scenic tour on their way to the ground. Thirteen gorgeous quail, a covey, marched aristocratically into view on the pine-needled duff of the circle of woods just beyond where I sat.

How brown and fine-feathered were the squat birds. The blue jay tapped the oaks, spilling leaves and acorns.

I did not want to go into the house. But tomorrow my mother would arrive for a week's visit. And I had to cook a pot roast, bake a cake, make a pie, clean the house, freshen the guest bedroom, and do some ironing.

But first, I would water my pot plants and flowerbed of orange and umber marigolds.

GROWTH

THIS IS the part that is hard to tell. Why, I'm not sure.

It isn't because it is painful for me to speak of it. Not that at all. It's only that I cannot be sure I am not getting the cart before the horse. Or the egg before the chicken. Or, was the chicken there which laid the egg which was there before the chicken.

It is a matter of precedence. Not of the lump. Once it was there, it got going rather rampantly. The most important subject of which I speak is that of the spirit.

Not my spirit. But the Spirit within.

It is the spirit which I had discovered "without." There outside me in all those woods, pervading and filling my very soul, the Spirit of God which was outside. Yet, the outside spirit was the inside spirit. It dwelt with me, even as it dwelt without me.

And that is where the difficulty lies for me in explaining. At what point did the Spirit within me make itself so felt, so manifested as to "altarize" my mind and intellect to deal as unequivocally as I did with this mass, this growth.

Certainly the groundwork had been laid in the progression of the past six months. The move into the woodlands which had pressed on me the imprint of the presence of God's spirit.

The illness and death of Jim. My coming to know beyond doubt, at least for me, that morning as I wrote in my journal and read from God's word as I sat at the wood's perimeter, that our spirit and soul are unending, that we are one with the Father through our belief in Jesus Christ.

From the beginning to the eternal.

And now, I knew during that week while my mother visited me, that the growth in my ribcage was larger. That I would have to go back to my doctor who, by now, had returned from his vacation.

What with Jim's death, and the arrival of relatives for the funeral, their stayover, and departure, my time had been full and busy. I had not gone for a further read-out of the X-ray results before my doctor's return, as he had suggested I do.

And then my mother arrived to spend a week. And I was so glad to see her. I chose not to go back to my doctor until after my mother had returned home. I did not mention it to her. With her hypertension and glaucoma, she did not need the jolt of knowing I had a growth to deal with. Worry would conceive itself and grow inside her. With no way to undo the worry.

Perhaps I did her an injustice. Her faith is great. She would have put her trust in God, in His goodness. But because of her physical ailments, I chose not to add worry, the insidious burrower.

But bath time and the mirrored-wall were a reminder that, ever so little at a time, the growth was enlarging.

The night before my mother would leave, I stood

there and looked at my rib area. I looked at it long and hard and firm.

And that's the way the protuberance was. Firm and hard. And three times the size it was when I had first noticed it. The rib seemed awry, protruding, which was what had caught my slight attention in the first place, almost four weeks ago.

Only now, much more so. And it was causing me discomfort. Not pain, but a constant drag of discomfort. I would know pain later. One day, I *had* known an excruciating few moments of pain. It was the week after all the family had left following Jim's funeral.

I was carrying a hamper of clothes down to the laundry. I turned the bend of the down stairway and the sharp end of the bannister hit me dead-center in the lump. There in the house alone, I screamed loud enough to raise the roof.

While my mother was there, we visited Joyce, went browsing, walked in the woods, sat by the creek. And felt the immensity of nature's enfoldment.

We peeped out at the raccoon, at the possum, in their nightly feedings outside the kitchen windows. One day the raccoon surprised us. He appeared at the peak of midday.

"That's the noon coon," said our son-in-law who was visiting.

Now, on Saturday morning, we stood on the roof deck at the airport. We saw the plane disappear into the remote clouds. It was carrying my mother back to Atlanta.

As we returned to our home in the woods, I did not mention the lump to my husband. He knew about it. But I went straight to the phone in our bedroom and called my doctor's office. I made an appointment to see him on the following Tuesday.

In those three days, from Saturday morning to Tuesday afternoon, I faced my situation squarely, as was necessary.

How simple that sounds. I think of the words of Job 16:16, *"On my eyelids is the shadow of death."*

I remembered the words of the Psalmist, *"The Lord is my strength and my shield; my heart trusteth in Him, and I am helped"* (Psalm 28:7).

How could I *trust* and not act, not do the thing that revealed my trust? I truly trusted God, and His love for us as revealed in his Son Jesus Christ. I knew, without doubt, that my heart would be filled with joy—even in this experience. His Holy Spirit would comfort me. And those I loved.

And I sought His word in the Book. The scriptures in the now-worn leather Bible my husband had given me for Mother's Day in the very springtime of our marriage.

How many years I'd turned its tissue pages, reading, studying. Its cover was so cracked, at times I was self-conscious about it. Yet holding it dear because of the words it held for me, and holding it dear because my beloved had given it to me.

And yet, one Sunday, a woman classmate in Sunday School said suddenly to me: "Virginia, when I see your Bible on your lap, or in your hands, it seems so *used,* and it gives me a feeling that you've lived close to God with that book. Just looking at your worn Bible does something to me."

I saw the words, *"Cast thy burden upon the Lord, and He shall sustain thee"* (Psalm 55:22).

And the voice of our Lord and Savior, *"My peace I give*

unto you . . . Let not your heart be troubled, neither let it be afraid" (John 14:27).

I read the words of Mark 11:24, *'Therefore I say unto you, what things soever ye desire, when ye pray, believe that ye receive them, and ye shall have them."*

I listened to the quiet voice of God within me. I felt the presence of God. His spirit. The presence of Christ within me.

* * *

I cannot describe it other than to say that there was not a vestige of fear. That to me was the miracle.

Yet, with the miracle of my calm, and my belief that God was with me, that no matter what, only good would come from whatever I was experiencing and would experience, the largest miracle to me was the miracle of acceptance.

Not resignation.

Acceptance. Reassuring acceptance.

I faced the fact that I had a lump. It might be benign. It might be malignant. I did not know.

But I was not afraid.

And I made the decision that I wanted to live with facts. With reality. Not fantasy.

* * *

My doctor's face reflected large surprise at the increase in the size of the growth.

I had already surmised that I would have to go into the hospital. For tests, at least.

My doctor confirmed this. I was not surprised.

"But with one understanding," I said to our long-time family doctor, surgeon, friend. "I want to know the score. The past year I've seen the death of my brother-in-law from cancer. The word was avoided and never mentioned. I want to live life on my terms. I want to face reality head-on. No matter what. I expect the best. But I want to know the score."

My doctor said softly, for he is a very human and compassionate person, "You will have the truth."

* * *

I would go into the hospital the next day, Wednesday afternoon.

In my beloved worn Bible that Wednesday I read the words in James 5:15, *"And the prayer of faith shall save the sick, and the Lord shall raise them up."*

THRESHOLD

THE MOST jubilant exultation of birdsong seems to come following the heavy rains. The earth has been drenched; all is soggy, dripping, absorbing. Then the wet look is no more. Cleaned, washed, laved. And calm the woods.

Then suddenly, the glory woods. Bursting with music. Resounding with jubilation. The trilling, la-la-ing of the woodthrush high among the bays, poplars, magnolias which rise from the lowlands. Unendingly pervading. Trills and ripples of ecstatic delight. Essences of joy, spilling in cascades, fountaining, splashing in all directions. Now in a soprano treble, now in an alto tribble, tribble.

The staccato richocheting of the clapper dapper red-bellied woodpecker in the upper hillside woods of oaks and persimmon and sassafras, singing his insistent trip-hammer song.

A bobwhite coming in clear and in fine tune. The bird's scissored call to his love, "Bob-White . . ." Then that echoing "Bob-White" faint, from the distance. The redbird's preening, "Prett ee, Prett ee . . ."

A granddaddy long legs spider moves trippingly across the concrete floor of the patio to hug the brick wall. Squirrels in the treetops going "wah-wah-wah," fidgeting for me to put out cracked corn for them and then to go inside so they can eat it. A brown rabbit coming round the corner of the house, seeing me, turns tail and off into the woods. . . .

All in fine feeling, reconciliation. Even the raucous blue jay brings joy.

And I sit on my upland hillside patio in the middle of it all.

Peace. The joy woods. The glory.

* * *

I would go into the hospital at 3 P.M. that day. But now it was 8 A.M. And John had gone to work.

I had asked him to do so, feeling that it would be easier on him and on me too, not to have to pass the morning away with "this" hanging between us. He would return in the middle of the day and we would have lunch, then drive in to the hospital.

I sat on the patio after he left. Feeling, seeing, being. A squirrel nibbled acorns in an oak above me. Then leaped to a tall pine. I looked up and saw the pine twinkling in early sun dazzle, redbirds in its boughs, silhouetted against the pale sky.

My heart was full. There were so many things I wanted to think about. John's brother's death and what it did to me.

It was as though infinity had somehow tapped through to me and I was for the first time in my life a *whole* person. The woodlands had taken me by the hand and led me into the presence of the Divine. It was as if something had been leading me all of my life to this place.

I thought of all the mornings after John had left for work, that I had gone into the woods. And down by the small stream towered over by bays and poplars, pines and maples. To sit and be and feel and absorb.

Sights: rabbits, squirrels, redbirds, blue jays, woodpeckers, mockers, thrashers, whippoorwill, raccoons, possum. . . .

And sounds: needles of pines spiraling, footfalls of squirrels, covey of wood-walking quail, crash of a pine cone, rustling of brown thrashers, and crackle of wind through hand-clapping trees, maples and poplars.

Always the trees, enfolding me, giving me comfort and love and acceptance. Always the woods, early and late.

I thought of that singular morning after Jim's death, when with that sudden clarity I *knew*.

For each of us it begins, they now say, at conception. But the larger mechanics of clarifying must be begun somewhere by each of us . . . the assemblings of small understandings of a lifetime into a large knowledge that shapes and defines itself.

And what I had felt that morning seemed to be a sudden summation of awareness. I had felt peace. The peace that passeth understanding. For me it had come in the glory woods.

What we are is with us wherever we are. Yet there come the revelations that put a different light on things. The insights reached in sudden flashes of illumination. Staggering insights. Momentary signalings of immortality in the monotonous, the commonplace, the constant.

It is there in those split-suddenesses that our souls are revived: when there comes understanding, and courage.

My mother had visited and now gone. And now I was going into the hospital. But I was at peace. And committed to God.

It would affect others, but it was my problem.

To tell or not to tell my mother and our two children in distant states.

I feared the knowledge of possible tumor surgery would affect my mother adversely. You don't dally with glaucoma and hypertension. She would have worried. She couldn't have helped it. And it would have affected her blood pressure. So that was my decision. Not to tell.

With Kitty and Jerry, it was a matter of sparing them what I considered unnecessary worry.

I did not want them told beforehand of possible surgery with the implied suspense of malignancy. I did not want them going through the upset at a distance. That is a painful anguish. To be at a distance . . . far far away . . . Colorado and California . . . not knowing and agonizingly caring. I wanted to spare them that. That was my decision, not to tell them beforehand.

I would tell them later. In my time. In my way. John was reluctant not to let them know. But I made him promise.

The strange, or not so strange, thing was that I knew I would be all right. Whether cancer was there or a benign growth, I knew there would be good within the entire experience. And so, since I was serene, trustful and not worried, I did not want the chimera of concern hovering on those I loved who lived so far away.

Sitting there on the patio that morning with all these things walking quietly through my mind, I knew suddenly that I must go inside the house. That I must go into my study and write a letter to the person I have loved most in all my life. My husband.

With all my internal and spiritual assessment, I had not been able to speak with my husband of the clarity I had found. I had been unable (perhaps like Jim) at that time to speak of the depths which enveloped me. The profound feelings had been kept within. And I needed to share them with him. More than that, I wanted to offer him some form of comfort. For I knew his unspoken anguish for me.

And so, I wrote a letter.

Dear John,

Perhaps if I say this it may make the upcoming ordeal a bit easier for you.

I know, without your telling me, that you are suffering for me. And that you love me. And that you would do anything you can to help me. I know all this. I thank you. And I love you.

But the fact is, we each have to experience our own suffering. You in your way. I in mine. That is just the way it is.

It helps me to know that you love me.

I face each day as this day. No more. No less. We live in each day. And however ill or well we do it, that is where we are living.

I have faced this thing head-on. It is not easy. It will not be easy. But I am facing it. I am trusting in God. In his love. In his infinite mercy.

I hope it will not be malignant. I pray it won't. But if it is, then that is simply another fact that must be faced and lived with as long as possible.

Jim's experience gave me much strength. Sort of a legacy. Each of us, in a way, I suppose, gives a legacy to someone or other.

Perhaps I'm saying this poorly. But I wanted you to know that I am deeply conscious of your concern and your love.

And grateful for it. My heart brims with love for you and with joy for all the good that life has brought me.

Jenny

We drove to the hospital that day exactly one month to the day since Jim died.

Just before we left for the hospital, I went up to our beautiful bedroom with the double glass doors looking onto the dogwood branches. So often here together we had looked down into the deep woods, heard the singing little stream in the night as we lay on our bed. As we had known the enfolding presence of the woods that throbbed with love.

I laid the letter on John's pillow.

PRE-SURGERY

THE NEXT MORNING, Thursday, I woke up at 4:30 A.M. I was lying in my hospital bed, wide awake. I turned on the bedlight. Then, with unbreakable habit, I reached for my journal and pen. From the background of my newspaper reporting days, I thought, "No time for re-writes."

It's as simple as that, Lord. That moving finger must write it the first time around, clearly, truly, purely.

Think it, feel it, pen it. No time for re-writes.

Last night at 8:30 the doctor said, "We'll have to explore this thing, Virginia."

You explore it your way, dear doctor.

I'll explore it mine.

Each with his own instrument.

Your scalpel.

My pen.

Both guided by the same Spirit.

God.

And time. That tumor grew in those four weeks.

Lord, when I go home there is writing to be done. Whatever that surgery is tomorrow, it must be done, taken care of, gotten out of the way so that I may get on with the writing.

I expect you to get me through it, dear Lord, in fine style, your child of faith. How thankful I am for those seventeen years of teaching Sunday School lessons to those little seven-year-old boys and girls. The repetition of teaching them in simple language grounded *me* in your Word. How your words appear to me in magic moments as golden shibboleths. (What's a shibboleth, Lord?)

But I expect you to get me through this ordeal, Lord. Yes, it's an ordeal, isn't it.

You've gotten me through other ordeals, Lord. My faith wasn't as fixed, as steady, as sure as now.

But it was the best I could do at the time.

You knew that. Didn't you, Lord?

Faith is like anything else.

It has growing pains.

Yet, even if it takes us all the way to the last to get it sure and steady and firm, why, that's something.

Isn't it, Lord.

But no matter how painfully, I expect you to get me through this.

And back to the marvelous woods.

And to the writing.

That's your talent, Lord, moving in me. Not mine. And I must be at it with surety. For now, there is no time for re-writes.

5:30 A.M.

Again, I awoke at 4 o'clock the next morning, Friday, after a deep-seated sleep, drug-induced. I almost went back to sleep, but decided to write an overdue letter to a writer friend, long ago moved to California.

I felt about her, as I do all writer-friends. That they are jewels, gems and rock-granite substances.

A nurse, wonderful and so human, came in. She discovered me thus engaged at 4:15 A.M. Pitch black dark outside.

She gave no remonstrations or tch-tch-ing, but a beautiful offer: "Would you like some coffee?" Imagine. At 4 A.M.

Letter finished, I got up and did my ablutions, put on fresh pajamas and felt fresh.

I read the Bible, absorbed, and thankful, in praise for the day, for my doctor, and for the NOW and what lay ahead. These were my spiritual ablutions bringing freshness of the soul.

Peace. Joy. Commitment.

I added water to the jar of red roses John brought me last evening. The dawn was paling in. I could see twin-eyed car lights flowing down Louiselle Street to the valley of the Infirmary. Workers arriving for the 7 A.M. shift.

Car lights faded. Yellow daisies and purple ageratum smiled at me in the bouquet in my room, sunshine from my daughter and son-in-law's backyard.

Another nurse came in to talk with me, "to chat." All who came through my doorway seemed inordinately kind, not hygienic sterile computers. Human. They overflowed with care and concern, and shared themselves with me whenever I asked a question. And their openness was startling.

I wondered, is it me? Or them?

Sudden thought.

Maybe "Tumor on chest wall" written on my patient chart makes a difference.

I go to surgery at one o'clock.

POST-SURGERY

SUFFERING MOVES in the small hours of the night, down the chambered corridors. The suffering that knows no words, only groans, moans, sounds, half-cries cut short in gasps, like smoke rings rising from a briar pipe, steady one atop another, blending, extending.

The wild dreams I had three nights in a row were trying to tell me something.

I was too weak to write about them. I remembered waking up once in the recovery room under the blinding lights, hearing my doctor say to me as he moved backward and forward in blurred vision:

"We had to re-sect a rib, Virginia, but we got it all."

Got what? I remembered no more.

But the dreams . . . I tried to bring them back. They were taking place days after my surgery.

The first dream, so vague, of earth. Of devastation, bottom lands with tree stumps, no trees, only stumps like cypress knees . . . gray, shadowy, no life.

The second dream was of water, everywhere water, everywhere flooded, tops of roofs showing, tips of trees, everything innundated. And moving along, riding on the water on some kind of inflated raft, there I moved along. Pushing along, helped by some kind of paddles.

The third dream transfixed and held me in sway. I was constructing a bi-plane, of wire and brown woodsy fabric. The plane was important for some one; someone was to fly it.

I was not sure how to construct it. I was uncertain. But I proceeded as if I knew exactly what to do and how to do it. I was certain I did not know how, but I was doing it with confidence.

Then, there was this person, or other force, or whatever, in the finished bi-plane, with its wings and tail and open cockpit. And I knew then that my uncertainty would somehow be resolved.

That while I had known it was for someone to fly, I had not truly felt the person was inside the plane flying and leaping and sailing.

And then the most marvelous vision began.

The plane began doing splendid loop-de-loops, climbing upward, arching in backward, and dipping, rolling easily and airily like a bird.

All in a deep deep tall tall forest of crimson and gold and brown and green leaves, never hitting nor touching the limbs and boughs, but gliding up and down and in and through and around in a splendor of freedom and movement in that glorious autumnal splendor—beyond words.

I can still see the bi-plane gliding in rolling loops, high among the richly burnished leaves, flames and yellows, copper and bronze and gold of God's glory woods.

I had the strong feeling that the wild dreams had been telling me something. Finally, the dreams fashioned a conclusive sentence in my mind:

The desired accomplishment must be built into the

planning and creation and execution as if it were already achieved. It must exist as if the achievement already exists before it is begun. And the key word was . . . trust.

* * *

Mabel came to visit. The troubled friend of mine whom I had not seen in over a year. I was now improved. Perishably weak, but re-alerted, free of that awful night-day hurt from the wound incised by my ministering surgeon. The wound now healing, slowly but certainly at its own pace.

I welcomed with joy a careworn friend who, on her lunch hour, had come to cheer me.

I was improved "vastly," as I told my doctor, even as I reeled in weakness. But I no longer hurt with anguish, so I was better. And my friend was beset. I could tell.

"I'm better," I said in true delight. (True delight is not to have hurt in the night.)

"Now tell me . . ." I said. I knew what to ask of my troubled friend. And she told me about her life's problems. I nodded.

Again I said, "Now tell me of . . ." Friends know friends and what to ask.

And she spilled out, spelled out, poured forth. And we communed.

"God loves you," I said. "You are as worthy as those you serve. Don't lose sight of your own worth on earth."

It was no sick room.

It was a room of healing. The nights were the worst. One was particularly terrible. But healing was going on in the midst of pain.

I had known that inrushing touch that comes from God, that flows into us, envelops and enfolds.

My friend and I smiled. And loved each other with our smiles. Mine was weak, but grateful and joyous in the wonder of healing.

* * *

On Thursday, October 19, seventeen days after I entered the hospital, I wrote a thank-you note to "my church."

> *Dear Church Family,*
>
> *I've always believed in prayer. But to be prayed for personally, to feel that wave of love, that mighty force of love, so gentle, so powerful,*
>
> *Embraced by love, prayers, thought, wish—I knew them all from you, my church family.*
>
> *Part of a rib is missing, but so much more has been added to me by your love and God's.*
>
> *After radiation, now pending, I expect to leave the hospital and go home to the woods on Saturday.*

CANCER-FACING

CANCER. Radiation.

Strange, the things that throw us. Incongruous things.

It wasn't the cancer that was throwing me. Nor the fact that I would have to undergo radiation, cobalt treatments.

For the first three shadowy pain-filled days and nights following the surgery, nothing had been on my mind except to "go through" the pain. Some things can't be by-passed. They must be gone through. And I meant to "get through" the pain.

But one glaring absence hit me in those days and nights when my husband and daughter and son-in-law ministered to me. *Not one* of them said to me in my lucid moments:

"It wasn't malignant."

The absence of those words informed me that the tumor had been malignant. This did not fret me. Getting through the pain was my goal.

But on the third day, or thereabouts, when my doctor was removing the drainage tube, I said,

"When can we talk?"

"Right now, if you want to," he said.

Then he told me in language I don't much recall except that the tumor was "as large as a hen's egg." A malignant lymphoma. It had not gotten into the lung. "Resecting" a rib had enabled them to "remove all of it, intact."

"You may have to have radiation treatment," he'd said then. "We'll talk about that later. I defer to the radiologist in that area."

The "later" came, and it was throwing me.

I would have to have cobalt treatment *every day* (except Saturday and Sunday) for *four weeks.* I had thought maybe once or twice a week.

The problem of greater magnitude was the fact that I had to get transportation to the woods each day from the hospital. Twelve miles.

After I went home from the hospital, I could ride in with John each morning as he went in to work. He could drop me off at the hospital (thud, thud, when someone drops you off).

This prospect of finding transportation confronted me even before I went home from the hospital. I just didn't know what to do about it.

Then a friend visited me in the hospital. I shared my problem with her. She said:

"Virginia, why don't you call your church?"

It was so simple. I never would have thought of it.

I called our young minister of education. "Bill, I have a problem. Do you think there are some ladies in the church who might like to take me on as a 'missionary project?'"

He said, "I'll check up and find out. I'm sure we can work out something."

That is how I became a missionary project. It was a far-reaching, friendship-forming experience.

The women in the adult (male and female) Sunday School class to which I belonged, organized themselves around me. With schedules organized for which one would pick me up at the hospital each morning. I was bowled over to learn later there were so many that they actually were vying for the opportunity to serve.

For three weeks. The fourth week, I struggled with my old gearshift Ford and did it on my own. I would groan and clutch my incision when I wasn't clutching the Ford. But glad I could manage.

And each morning I would have—as I called it—my three minutes of tranquility on the cobalt table. Lying there beneath the huge machine's well-trained gun peering down on my resected rib area. The bandage was still on during the first week. The radiologist would touch me gently on my undraped shoulder (a pillow case covered my indifferent bosom), smile and say as he departed the room:

"Think happy thoughts."

I always did. I could feel that massive monster of a darling machine above me, penetrating, technologically transmitting the abundance of God's healing, touching and entering and filling the affected areas. Then the sudden "thrummmmp" that always startled me. And that little faint "hummmmmmmm" before it signaled halt.

With the female technician assisting, I quickly pulled my slip up from where it had been shoved waistward, my arms through the straps, and put on my blouse and jacket. I was already wearing my skirt and undergarments. I was going bra-less. It had nothing to do with Women's Lib. An aching chest area couldn't bear the pressure.

I quickly got out so the next tranquil patient could

111

enter. For actually, it was an assembly line of healing (and thrummmmping and hummmmmming).

Unendingly, they came, with all kinds of cancers. In the cobalt waiting room, you came to know and feel a kind of cancer camaraderie. People smiled, some spoke, some commented on how they felt. As one walked through the doorway, you smiled a silent welcome. If he were a regular, the hello's or good-mornings were almost simultaneous.

Lymphomas, melanomas, choose a name. They're not the same, all those cancers. They're different, finite, varying, variable. Yet we in the waiting room are unified in having come to grips with reality.

The elderly, in wheel chair, or carrying a cane. It never occurred to me to think, "Wonder what he has," or "she has." Somehow we were all lumped together under that umbrella designation. Cancer.

The closed circle ever opening to admit new ones. The new ones of those 665,000 new cases that would be diagnosed (for the first time) in 1973.

A frog-throated woman said one morning, "I'm scared."

I said, "Don't be afraid. It will help you."

She smiled a wobbly smile. "I'm not as scared as I was yesterday, my first time."

They were treating her for cancer of the larynx, with radiation before surgery. Others were there, post-surgery as I, with follow-up radiation.

But the difference in the people in the waiting room —even the walls felt it—was that each recognized in the other that fact, "Here's where it's at. We've got a serious problem. You . . . I . . . all of us here. And we're dealing with it. We're not pretending it doesn't exist. When we come here, we manifest that it does exist. And we're dealing. And coping."

The difference within that waiting room was that when you met someone's eyes, that person met yours. And smiled. There was no sudden averting of the eyes' meeting, as in most doctors' waiting rooms. That refusal to acknowledge the fellow-human-beingness of the one who looked. Always the averting of the eye.

Within the cobalt waiting room, there was the acknowledged bareness of our souls. Nobody tried to hide. We were revealed human beings. Trying very hard to become more human—before we, for many would—became no longer mortal.

There I learned that understanding is to be had with the open eye. The averted eye denies. The opened eye, as with the opened heart, takes in, learns, augments. Even if part of it is dying. Yet, living even more fully in the dying.

The woman who came from a distance, who had to find a rooming house in town, and take a cab to the radiation therapy of the hospital. Who said she "looked to God and He heard and answered."

The man who was sitting there, from his home 75 miles away.

With his friend sitting beside him. His friend who drove him daily, 75 miles. He said, "I've come to know you have to depend on friends."

He learned something I was discovering.

One day, one of my friends, the ones who were "carting" me home each day, said to me: "Virginia, I know this must be very hard on you. You are such an independent person."

I smiled broadly at her.

"Quite the contrary. It is such a beautiful experience for me. I am so thrilled by the love displayed in these acts of kindness to me, that I accept it with the love with which it is being offered. I have no pride. Only gratitude."

I had come to know that in my accepting, openly and with warm gratitude, these rides—which surely caused some inconvenience and revamping of home schedules —my acceptance was in itself a gift of love to them. It was a mutual reciprocity of undisguised love.

Some of the women who drove me home, I knew fairly well. Others, only from a smile or comment on Sunday morning from one or the other of us before the class began. It was a very large class, and I did not know everyone in it. And we had no contact as a group, except Sunday mornings.

Some were high society. Such a quaint phrase that dates me. Yet applicable in this deep South city. Some were strugglers, along with me. On Sunday morning we were all leveled in the house of God.

And each morning at the hospital there would be one to greet me. Smilingly, openly joyous to be of help to me, looking forward to our 12-mile chat. Visiting over a cup of coffee (ready at the flick of a switch when we got there). And perhaps a walk into the woodlands down by the stream . . . in the crispy sunny November weather . . . we were leveled by love.

Spoken intimacies within the steel-enclosed womb of a car, cars by degrees fancy and unfancy, the 12-mile intimacy, formed friendships that to this day retain their viability.

A member of one woman's family had had a cancer

operation. And still panicked at the faint hint of any protuberance.

Some talked of their children, college age or high school age. Some of preparing a great meal on that evening for some important client of their husband. We shared vissicitudes as women.

Yet it always came round to cancer. They were interested and looked to me for some clue.

Shall we discuss it—go on, say it, cancer. Or shall we avoid it, skirt it, knowing it exists but pretending that somehow, it wasn't the cause of the gift of a ride.

This wasn't spoken. But it was inherent in the friendly smile and sometimes too hearty manner. And so, to put them at ease, I gave them a clue. Each time.

We discussed how it came about, my feelings about it, above all, the fact that it was not a taboo subject if they wanted to talk about it. It did not hog the conversation. But it was approached, treated, dealt with, gotten out of the way. Then more immediate and current interests of each of us were gotten into.

Sometimes religious. Sometimes philosophical. Sometimes comical incongruities. We rollicked and regaled and laughed and talked ponderously of things so deep and powerful that sometimes we would be both amazed that such depths were coming from each of us.

And then we'd laugh. For we knew that no one else would believe that each of us was as deep as we were proving ourselves to be. And on each instance, the revelation was as wonderfully refreshing as that first washing-over stupendous mountain of a surging-in wave on the beach. Exhilarating.

No missionary anywhere on any field in God's world

ever felt more uplifted, upheld and benefited by any project of missionary-minded people back in the home churches than I did during those three weeks.

There was something else I learned. Or partly. How to deal with cancer. Your own. Or someone else's.

You take a clue from the person who has it. You do not avoid it. You simply wait for some hint as to whether it is a taboo subject or not.

You do not avoid visiting someone who has had a cancer operation simply because you do not know what to say or do. (I had done this.) The recuperating patient needs contact with others. Loving, caring contact.

I remember a dear friend of mine who had lived next door to us years ago. She had a radical mastectomy four years ago. I knew it. I never went to see her. I felt uncomfortable when I thought of her, because she had . . . go on, say it . . . cancer. Not because, specifically, it was breast cancer, but just cancer.

There are all kinds of reactions in the process of dealing with a cancer situation. When the prognosis is good. When it is indeterminate. And when it is bad.

Yet in every case, it is dealt with by the patient. Either by facing it. Or avoiding it.

To our knowledge, Jim was never told that he had cancer following his last operation, for gall bladder removal. (He'd had three operations.) It was as if he did not want to be told. Likely, his doctor took his cue from Jim. Doctors have to do this.

I believe Jim knew he had cancer. His father died with it. His brother died with it. I believe he knew he had it. Yet mention of it was avoided. It was this way until he died.

So, that's the way we dealt with it when we visited him.

We inquired of how he felt, and listened when he told us.

Yet, I should not have avoided my friend. When she and her husband came to visit us after my husband's subsequent heart attack, she and I talked.

And I told her of my feelings and why I had never come to see her during her recuperation. I simply felt too uneasy. But I told her that I had learned that you can visit and you can take a cue from the patient, recovered completely or not.

The most important thing I learned as a cancer patient, I think, is that it is of enormous kindliness to the visitor that you relieve him of his unease and help him feel comfortable with you (even if you are uncomfortable).

HOME AGAIN

THE DAY THAT I went home from the hospital after seventeen days' stay, I walked into our house on my own two feet. That evening I prepared supper for John and me. I was able to do it. But I groaned a lot. My ribcage kept reminding me of its presence.

Our telephone rang that evening. (Ah, blessed sound.) It was our son Jerry, who lives in California. I had intended to write to him the next day and tell him of my operation, the entire story. I told him now, on the phone.

He listened. Then he was very silent. He said finally, in a very low voice,

"Well, Mother, knowing you, I can't see how you would have handled it any other way, not telling us beforehand."

With Kitty, in Colorado, it was the same. The next day I wrote to her. I explained that her Daddy was afraid that she would be hurt with him for not telling her about the surgery, or that I was in the hospital. But that I had made him promise to wait. She understood.

But both Kitty and Jerry asked now that I send them progress reports.

* * *

The woods were turning redder and more golden.
More glorious. I had missed a near three-week gap of
them and they now enfolded me unto themselves
through windows and glass doors.

One morning as I sat at the kitchen table after John
had gone to work, the quail appeared. Plump and elegant, they flowed from the underbrush one by one, thirteen of them, moving in that archly dignified flowing
movement. They had come to breakfast with me. There
at the cracked-corn feeding ground of the daytime squirrels, redbirds, the nighttime picnic ground of the possum, rabbits and raccoons.

The browns and blacks of their feathers blended into
the beiges and whites of stripes on their heads. The
beige stripes denoted the female, the white stripes sig-
nified male.

I sat there, spellbound by the feathery commune.
Watching that fast footwork of scratching as the head is
raised momentarily to give the look of unconcern even
as the foot scratches, raking the grain for quick gobble.
They would move in jerky fluidity at some crackle of
danger, dart into wood's edge, spread out in isolated
spots like hidden Easter eggs, stone still.

Then, at some leadership signal, they came back together into one unit, the family.

I had become fascinated in reading about the quail. I
had learned that the female hatches two setting of eggs
during a year. And that the male quail cares for the
young of the first hatching while the female quail hatches
the second batch. I found this father-caring immensely
appealing. And in the fall, they all came together as the
commune.

I had read of the simultaneous response of the entire covey to a danger signal. Of their instant stillness at such a signal. Of the quick freeze. So strong was this response to danger that if the threatening sound or animal persisted, the entire group as a unit remained still. They had been known to stand, immobile against heard danger, even as falling rain turned into sleet, into ice and they had literally become frozen as a group.

The new world which had opened up for me out in the woods had forced me to do research on my nature neighbors. I was inveterately curious about them. I like my human neighbors. But I was seldom curious about their doings. Certainly not to the point of doing research on it!

By now, I was able to do most of my housework. I groaned a great deal as I made the bed and washed the dishes. I did not brandish the vacuum cleaner yet. But I was so glad to be able to do what I did.

I had forced myself through those mornings of getting breakfast for John and me very early, to go to the hospital for the cobalt treatment each morning.

I dreaded engaging myself in the gearshifting, rib-cramping driving of myself to the hospital and back.

Now, my strength would flag about noon and I would rest for a period, then be up and working again. So far, there were no side effects from the radiation treatment. My pain consisted of natural healing processes, nerves, neuritis and spasms.

It was over a month since I had left the hospital, then the four weeks of cobalt treatment, that machine with its noises. I realized in retrospect that the noises had alternated between sounds of an old electric pump and fizzes of static on an old Atwater Kent radio.

The "treatment" was complete. Final X-rays and blood test showed "all clear."

Now a week, ten days had passed since the okay signal. And still, I could not bring myself to write about any of it in any of my notepads or journals.

People, friends, my physician-surgeon when I went for a check-up, all asked, "Any side effects from the radiation?"

"No," I would say. "It wouldn't dare."

But now—the small appearances of mild depression. I almost said "light depression." But there is nothing "light" about depression.

Small things triggered me. I was vulnerable, weak, and strength lasted only in brief periods.

That was the hardest thing to deal with. The weakness that left me victim to feelings which, otherwise, I could throw off.

I concentrated on my blessings. I said to myself, It could have been a leg amputation instead of a rib. I could have been left unable to get about with ease, unable to do my work.

I would think. I am mobile, ambulant, able to do my work, despite my acute discomfort.

But even the discomfort that came and went irritated me. I seemed to think it should go away instantly and stay gone. It never stayed gone. It came back. The ache in the incision area, the nerve ends hurting, the spasms and cramps of muscles that were sliced and trying to reknit.

My body was calling the cadence, the pace. And I kept forgetting that it must have its reins loose. I could not push it.

But I reached for hope wherever I could find it. I read. Oh, how I read.

One book was of especial interest to me. It dealt with body chemistry and the possible effect of the mind on matter, cells, their alteration and growth.

Even to the idea that wrong thought, destructive thought, can actually set up a chain of reaction resulting in cell growth into tumors. I had greatly dealt with this idea in my own mind, wondering if. . . .

I phoned the office of the American Cancer Society in our city. They mailed to me the fine large booklet containing "Cancer Facts and Figures" for the current year and the projected figures for the following year. (The booklets are available, and kept current. Any local American Cancer Society office can supply them. Or The American Cancer Society, National Headquarters, 219 E. 42nd Street, New York, New York 10017.)

And there was the then-current newspaper story of the boy, "dying of cancer," as the doctors said, who had been given drugs so strong that few patients survived the side effects.

Doctors could not explain the "remission," the dramatic reversal in his life. A four year battle, results of which the doctors could not explain.

The 13-year-old boy could explain it.

"God has a plan in my life," he said.

I read everything I could get my hands on about cancer, and how it is being dealt with in the scientific fields, both surgically, chemically, and in research.

I do not attempt to explain the healing of some cases of cancer and not in others. People more learned than I cannot explain it.

The answer rests with God.

But I remembered the "attitude of life" in Dr. Viktor Frankl's book, *Man's Search for Meaning.* I recalled the memorable account of psychiatrist Dr. Frankl's harrowing experiences in Nazi concentration camps. And how he voiced the certainty that ultimately one does have a choice, no matter how terrible the circumstance.

One can walk into the gas chamber cursing . . . or affirming God's love.

And the words of Proverbs kept coming in on me, "As he thinketh in his heart, so is he."

NOVEMBER'S WOODS

"LISTEN," said John one Saturday morning as we awoke. "Doves."

It was the gentle sound of cooing, coming from the front woods. A pair of doves, our newest of families, cooing morning and evening.

We walked our woodland circle in the morning. Saw squirrels dropping pine cones they were eating like corn-on-the-cob. Saw the flame of reds and golds in dogwood, maples and blackgum, picked a sprig of briar vine loaded with orange berries.

Berries of all kinds graced everything, on the ground, and in corsages on branches. There were purples of winter huckleberry, elderberry, scuppernong and reds of dogwood and wild youpon. We seldom picked them, even for bouquets, leaving them as delicacies for the birds.

I saw a worm-webbed willow in the marsh that looked as if it wore clouds in its hair.

We heard the studied call, "Juree, juree," of the towhees in the massive brushpile, as they frolicked in low swoops. And far in the distance, the tom-tom call of the woodpecker.

We stood beside the pond at the small dam and saw

minnows flocking to our cast bread like blue jays darting, grabbing, running, returning. Tiny brown, gray and larger striped ones. A small catfish appeared suddenly, causing the minnows to leap, jumping like mullet. The catfish scurried, probing the bottom. He disappeared beneath a rock in the dam.

A dragonfly flurried, skimming the water.

"What besides bread do minnows eat?" I wondered aloud.

"Plankton."

In this creek? Plankton?

A crawfish moved suddenly.

Sunlight danced on the water. Minnows swam upstream against the current, like little children doing battle with the waves.

At night, John and I walked down to the little pond-dam area, carrying large flashlights. We focused the beams on the waters, saw the catfish, and crawfish with the most amber eyes . . . one little surely newborn crawfish seemed to be all eyes, glowing amber, connected to a tiny tail and whiskers. Lined up like submarines and hovering on the bottom were three small trashfish. We called them pike, but we weren't sure.

And right in the middle of the small pond, there was the great old granddaddy snapping turtle. His gargantuan neck and head and powerful elephant-hided feet, plus that enormous shell covered with green moss always struck me with vision of prehistoric monster. Every time I came upon him in the water, the same vision assailed me. Prehistoric monster.

It did not comfort me to know that turtles have no teeth. For such a snapper can tear something with his jaws, even with no teeth.

I remembered one day when John had called me down to the pond. He wanted me to see a sight. And it was a sight. The huge snapping turtle was there in the middle of the pond. Between his jaws he held a snake, partially eaten, a long snake. It's belly was to the top, all white and pristine in the water, clamped between those jaws.

I thought of my big beautiful black snake that I had stalked and had so come to admire that brief time I followed him as he explored our home's perimeter down into the fern-fronded brushpile lowlands to disappear.

I hoped fervently it was not my beautiful black snake.

John had poked at the snapping turtle with a long pole sufficiently to make him let go of the snake.

"I want to see what kind of snake it is," he said.

He poled the snake out of the water onto the bank. It was not a snake. It was an eel.

He threw the eel back into the water for the turtle to recapture. I sighed thankfully that it was not my ambling friend, the black snake.

But I thought, "Poor eel."

We knew for a fact now that there were three snapping turtles traversing our woodland waters. A middle-sized turtle, lesser in size than this granddaddy. And a small snapping turtle, almost cunning looking, the size of a hand. The little fellow would climb up a heavy forked scuppernong vine that rose from the creek waters not too far from the patio outside the family room.

Daily, he would slowly travel that moss-covered rooty vine from the water up about six feet to the fork. There he would settle himself and await the sun which rested on him there and warmed him for hours. The moss on the vine was worn slick where the little turtle had made himself at home. It seemed hard to believe that the little tad could ever grow into that frightening looking creature that tenaciously grabbed onto the hapless eel.

At breakfast each morning, John and I dined with the redbirds and the squirrels. The squirrels with their tiny hands holding corn kernels, their stomachs showing white and fluffy as they sat upright, dining with us just a patio apart.

White-throated sparrows arrived one morning down from the North to winter with us. To breakfast, dine and sup with us daily, and to drink from nearby lowland waters. And one day a sight came we'd never seen before. Tiny little birds of the brightest blue imaginable. Indigo buntings.

And everywhere the glories of the woods, the trees, the flames and golds and wines and dubonnets of tonal reds. They danced and sang . . . and I thought of the words in Isaiah, "For ye shall go out with joy, and be led forth with peace: the mountains and the hills shall break forth before you into singing, and all the trees of the field shall clap their hands."

Surely the trees were clapping their hands and the hills were breaking forth into singing.

Peace. In these glory woods.

DECEMBER

DECEMBER CAME in on the tapestry of frost. I walked down to bid John farewell at the outer drive. As I waved to him, the frosted prisms of pinks and blues sparkling in the early morning sunlight caught my attention.

It was a spread-out pattern of frost-touched dewberry vines hugging the roadside edge. They trailed down the side of the road in the most dazzling artistry I'd ever beheld. Frost. Etched and embroidered in glints and glistens and snow-like crochetings of pale toned shadings that bound me in spell.

Hugging the dirt. Diamonds of rainbows, arcs and circles and pequoted edges. I had seen frost before. But never such a finished design of beauty in my life.

I clutched at my ribcage, binding it with the support of my left arm and walked my woodland circle back up to the house.

I was going to go Christmas shopping for our dears who live far away. Driving my gearshift, floor-clutching Ford still tied me in knots. But, if I sat back and refused to "go," that was stagnation, not living. So I would dole myself certain tasks each day, then urge myself forward until they were accomplished. All else went by the wayside.

I gait-paced my physical activity to the right ribcage's refusal to straighten up and fly right. I knew it would in time. Meanwhile, I would groan when it cramped and grabbed me in spasms, which was about one-third to one-half of the time now.

But life was precious and I lapped it up to the uttermost.

John had bought for me, as a Christmas present weeks before Christmas, a marvelous chair. A swivel rocker, recliner, covered in black leatherlike vinyl so soft it was almost satiny. Tapered and tufted, feminine, not bulky looking. Best of all, it just fit me. Or I fit it.

Throughout the day I would go to it, deposit myself gingerly. I say gingerly, for sitting was the hardest thing for me. Every ribcage is connected to the spine. And the spine is where you sit. Or thereabouts.

I would sit in the chair and gaze out the double glass doors of the family room. Into the at-hand forest of flame and golden maples, poplars and sassafras leaves.

I was never sure whether it was the chair, or the beholding that made me tranquil. But I would arise, renewed.

John had already put up Christmas outdoor lights across the first floor roof edge of the house. At night, as you drove past on the lower road, the lights looked like stars twinkling through the woods.

I set forth to do my Christmas shopping for the day. A certain number of purchases to be "gotten through." My energy lasted in short spells, so I took advantage of it.

After parking my car in the huge parking lot, I walked toward the heavy door leading to the shopping mall lobby. I looked about for a strong man who might open the door. No one in sight. Except, there, an older man shuffling up to the entrance. One arm was in a sling, and he inched along with the use of a metal cane in the other hand. I sized him up as possibly a stroke victim.

I realized suddenly that I was better off physically than he was. Without thinking twice, I reached for the long door handle and laboriously pulled it open. I thrust my body against it to hold it open so he could enter.

He smiled gratefully at me. "I have a hard time with doors," he said.

I smiled back. "Yes sir, I know what you mean. I do too. I've just had part of a rib removed because of cancer."

He looked stricken, that I had opened the heavy door.

"Oh, no," I said hastily, "I'm better, don't worry about it, I'm better."

His face eased its stricken look. "I'm glad you're better, I'm glad you're better." Like I was doing, he was repeating himself.

He shuffled on along. I did too. Realizing the stores would not open for ten more minutes, I went into Woolworth's cafeteria which was open. I slid into the booth. I was gasping long heaving gasps, trying to get relief from the spasms that had grabbed me vise-like from opening the door.

The waitress came up. Concern was in her voice as I tried to find my voice. "Are you all right?"

"I'm fine, I'm fine," I gasped. "I'll be all right." I ordered coffee and a scrambled egg and sat there. The spasms finally were easing.

Then I became aware of voices at a table just beyond me. "How many sugars you want in your coffee, sir?" a waitress with the softest voice was saying as she tore open the sugar packets, pouring sugar into the cup, then stirring it. "Oh, I've waited on you before, sir."

The man, for it was he for whom I'd opened the door, and his back was to me, must have commented on her kindness to him, for she said in a sweet and ringing voice:

"Oh, yes, sir. I try. As long as I am alive. As long as I am alive."

I came then to the conclusion that we all repeat ourselves when we are attempting to make sure that someone understands our true feelings, that we are being understood.

Later that morning I went into a rest room, backing into it, pushing the heavy door with my body. When I was leaving, a teen-ager reached to pull the door open for me. "Thank you so much," I said. "I'm having a hard time with doors." She immediately rushed ahead of me to open the door leading to the outside.

Perhaps it was because it was Christmas that I noticed it especially. Perhaps it was the larger combination, my own need for help, plus Christmas in the air, store fronts glittering, Salvation Army bells jingling.

Whatever it was, I assessed it as love. As man manifesting Christ, or trying to, in the Christmas season.

When I told my husband about it later, I summed it up, "There is so much kindness abroad. I never realized it, until I needed some of it myself."

He said quietly, "It's been there all the time."

SHARING

EACH OF US has friends who mean something special in our life. Della is such a friend to me. For years, we've shared our writing worlds.

And it was she who had invited me to attend with her the opening of the Providence Hospital Art Gallery. Where I had viewed the paintings of local artists. Where I had stood, transfixed, before a huge oil painting of "The Washerwoman." Transported back in time to a world of washboards and Octagon soap and raw knuckles and throbbing legs that caused you to sag with wash-day weariness.

Where I had yearned openly for a painting that so gripped and ached me, with its essence of quiet courage before the days of Woman's Liberation and Maytags. A painting that I could not afford. A painting that had set me to wondering about the forces rampant in artists. What made them paint? Were the forces the same that made a person write? So many things I wondered about the creative process.

And now, I was back in the woods, dealing daily with the recovery process of pain, and depression, all of which continued to lessen, but would not quite go away and stay away.

Then, one day a week before Christmas my doorbell rang. Della stood there. "Hi," she greeted me.

Then she turned to go back to her car, the door of which stood open. She pushed the front passenger seat forward and leaned across the back floor, struggling with a large object. She lugged it into the foyer and into the family room. She placed it on the floor as I closed the front door.

I walked into the family room and stared unbelievingly. It was "The Washerwoman." The painting I had gazed on and was so overcome by one evening almost three months before.

The painting that had stayed in my mind. As art will do. As I try to convince myself that words are able to do, once written.

I was overcome. Not alone by the painting that gripped me now in actuality. Not alone by the knowledge that the painting reposed in our own home.

But by the words my friend said to me in tones ever so low:

"This is an I'm-glad-you're-alive present."

* * *

Dear Sweet Mother,

Walking slowly around the circle of woods this morning after John left for work, I beheld the glory of even a gray and loomingly fog-touched height and depth of forest. Limitless cavern of deep and somber wood. Only eight months after we moved from the city to the woods.

It is strange. There is a Power in those moisture-laden still and silent woods, brook-splashed. So dark and green as to be

almost black. All color of autumn has departed, fallen in ano-
nymity beneath the lowland evergreen undergrowth. The power
and force that is there is not mute. But it is overwhelming in
its silence.

The motionless cavern draws me as much to it as does the
woodland when it is graced by sunbeams playing tag.

And as I walked, I thought of those I love who live afar.

I thought, how nice if Mother were here to share. To walk,
and sit, and stare. No high blood pressure, no weakness to
prevent her enjoying.

Then I thought, how silly. We are where we are. Living,
enjoying, partaking, where we are.

We do not say, oh, if so-and-so were so, or not so. We do
not hold back time. We are where we are.

We might as well wish that our grown children were back
as little ones. Maybe this is the eternal Christmas season wish.
That we and our spouses were in the Springtime of our lives,
in that time when everything was love and beautiful in our
memories.

But if all mothers' children were once again small, and
vibrating with mercurial energy, then all mothers themselves
would be tiny moppets.

And that wouldn't do.

All mothers (and daddies) would be scampering tots and
there would be no mommies and daddies.

Time moves. Or does it.

We move. And live. And change. And become.

So, if I walk a woodland circle, I think of you. I commune
with you.

And with each dear and distant one that I love. Where I am.
No attempt to hold back time or stay its steps. Just communing,

breathing the spirit of loving feeling across spaces that inter-
vene.

   It is somehow in the words of that song that fills the air so
often at this season, "Joy to the world, the Lord is come!"
   A happy Christmas to you, in Jesus dear and precious name.
                                                    Love, Jenny

THOUGHT AS ESSENCE

IT IS MID-JANUARY. I am sitting on the patio now—
7:30 A.M.—coat-wrapped and yellow-stole muffled, looking into the amazing wonder of the woods.

Every morning I walk the woodland circle in front of
the house, and move among the hand-clapping trees. I
move, slow of step and filled with inexpressible absorp-
tion.

I ache with wanting each person in the world to be able
to walk and feel and know the woods, and the presence
of God therein.

My mind and spirit are trying so very hard to pin it
down. To verbalize the past nine months and what they
have brought to me in quiet revelation.

We left our lifetime's home in the city and moved to
our rural home in the woods. We found ourselves isolated in the immensity, the density of forest, a whippoorwill's call away from the highway.

The woods imprinted its divine nature on me and I felt
renewed and close to God among the towering trees.

The death of a dear relative moved me deeply.

Cancer confronted me and I was forced to face it, to
face myself, to face God.

136

How do we come to an understanding about ourselves and God? A truly larger understanding.

I believe that God's grace is working in us.

God's grace. Love. He loves you. Accepts you. Comforts you. Strengthens you. God's grace.

Without a doubt, cancer was the most awesome experience of my life. As close as I had always felt to God, this encounter brought me closer than I would have believed possible.

I grope for words to define the indefinable. For words to pin down the un-pin-downable.

But if a thing can be experienced, it can be told. Even something as elusive as feeling. For at the point where feeling and reality intersect—at that point, expression is born.

Others have discovered self and God. Some of us discover God's power and love in sudden flashes wherever we are.

We come upon the eternals, each in our own way, led by the Spirit. And like snowdrops, snowflakes, myriad as they are, each one's discovery is dazzlingly unique. Each of us is his own realizer of God's infinite holiness.

* * *

The cotton candy fog that dimmed the upper tree heights is thinning now, slipping down and dissolving like tears of joy in the woodlands.

My teacup is empty. But not I.

I am filled, always and always by the presence of God in his loving kindness and mercy. For I know that my redeemer liveth. I know that God so loved the world that he gave his only begotten son, that whosoever believeth in him should not perish but have everlasting life.

And I know that the presence of Christ within us can become known anywhere. Everywhere. For each of us.

For me, it has taken place, and is taking place in the woods. The glory woods.